Morals and the Meaning of Jesus

Morals and the Meaning of Jesus

Reflections on the Hard Sayings

Nicholas Peter Harvey

The Pilgrim Press
Cleveland, Ohio

Originally published by Darton, Longman, and Todd, Ltd.,
London, as *The Morals of Jesus,* © 1991 by Nicholas Peter Harvey

Pilgrim Press edition published 1993
The Pilgrim Press, Cleveland, Ohio 44115

Cover design by Gene Harris

Printed in the United States of America
The paper used in this publication is acid free and meets the
minimum requirements of American National Standard for
Information Sciences-Permanence of Paper for Printed Library
Materials, ANSI Z39.48-1984

98 97 96 95 94 93   5 4 3 2 1

Library of Congress Cataloging-in-Publication Data

Harvey, Nicholas Peter.
    [Morals of Jesus]
    Morals and the meaning of Jesus : reflections on the hard
sayings / Nicholas Peter Harvey.
        p.   cm.
    Originally published: The morals of Jesus. London: Darton,
Longman, and Todd, © 1991.
    Includes bibliographical references.
    ISBN 0-8298-0947-3 (alk. paper)
    1. Jesus Christ—Ethics.   2. Jesus Christ—Words.
3. Freedom (Theology)—Biblical teaching.   4. Bible. N.T.
Gospels—Criticism, interpretation, etc.   I. Title.
BS2417.E8H38   1993
226′.06—dc20   94-41216
                                                   CIP

In memoriam

MARY FRANCES HARVEY
of
Drumdaff

Mulier Fortis

Contents

Contents

Prologue

There is a living word. I shall not speak it, but I may be the catalyst for your hearing it. The word itself is a flame, an incandescence. It burns at the very heart of this creation. It sears, it invites, it illuminates. It is sheer gift, striking awe. It is for you, it is to you, it is in you. Wake up!

Introduction

Books claiming to be about Christian morality are plentiful. This one springs from an uncomfortable sense, sharpened by experience in teaching theological students, that in one way or another most thinking about Christian morality blunts the cutting edge of the story of Jesus, to our very great cost. More positively, the book results from an inability to get certain 'hard sayings' out of my head and heart. How or in what sense do these strangely unforgettable sayings connect with the moral project of becoming fully human? What is suggested is that this connection can be grasped through the inter-relation of the sayings and the story of Jesus' life and death, which turns out to be our story in a distinctive sense here made explicit.

The gospel text, though not where the book begins, is the starting-point. It must be said at once that I am not directly concerned in this work with whether or not Jesus said certain things, a question to which biblical scholarship properly prohibits cast-iron answers. On the other hand, even the fullest acknowledgement of the creativity of the evangelists hardly suggests that anything goes in their telling of the story of Jesus, which is in any case inaccessible except through their words. At the same time it is probably a mistake, and certainly not to my purpose, to ask literalistic questions of the story.

Another consideration which likewise helps to free us, if we let it, from the idolatry of something called 'biblical truth' is the conclusion reached by some textual critics that there is not and never has been such a thing as 'the text' in an absolutely definitive sense. What we have is a distillation of traditions, oral and written, which developed and interacted in complex ways from the time of the earliest available evidence.

These perspectives open up less constricting bearings than formerly on the fact that the four gospels eventually became, and remain, authoritative reference-points for the living out of further chapters in the Christian story. Critics and exegetes have between them helped to free the text for us by pressing their questions, however much we may disagree with some of their conclusions. It is also worth emphasising that, despite the fears of some and the hopes of others when faced with critical considerations, it cannot be conclusively denied that memories of Jesus play a decisive part in the formation of the tradition. Memory and creativity, whether on the part of the evangelists or of later editors, do not by any means exclude one another.

Oddly enough, those who most insist on the uniformly revelatory status and historicity of everything in the gospels often seem not to give priority to questions of meaning. Likewise those most convinced that justice and peace, healing and reconciliation are univocal keynotes of gospel morality often appear innocent of any really stretching engagement with what the 'hard sayings' might mean. In both cases the meaning seems already to have been decided and so is not given space to reveal itself. The result is sub-Christian cliché rather than theological exploration, whether the polemic happens to be against sexual permissiveness, social injustice or whatever.

The gospel text can occupy a privileged place *in our listening.* This is a process quite other than that 'searching of the Scriptures' roundly condemned by the gospel itself as anti-life. Such searching sees in the text the container of life, as if life itself is found and stored in the words themselves. By contrast, receptive attention to the story can help to diagnose our condition, sifting us free from besetting ideologies and compulsively unregenerate and imprisoning behaviour-patterns. The purpose of this diagnosis and sifting is not condemnation, still less moral perfection in the image of an idealised fantasy-self. It is rather rebirth into a world of wonder and a community of hope.

It may help to offer a description of each of the book's four parts. Part One marks out the ground in a very preliminary way. Elements of autobiography are included here, as elsewhere, not for their own sake but as possible catalysts in the making of comparable connections between the gospel and others' stories. Part Two breaks open some categories which dictate widely held, but to my mind mistaken, assumptions about the kind of morality Jesus represents. Part Three expands on the main themes of the book in a set of reflections around particular sayings. Part Four, focusing more on the story than on the sayings, rehearses two of the book's central concerns, dishonour and loss.

I want to acknowledge the indirect but enormous contribution made between 1980 and 1987 by all members of the ethics classes at the Queen's Theological College, Edgbaston, Birmingham, and on the West Midlands Ministerial Training Course. The college council gave me a sabbatical term, during which the late Abbot of Douai, Dom Gregory Freeman, who had earlier preached my ordination retreat in what now seems like another age, gave crucial support at a fragile moment. Members of the Association of Teachers of Moral Theology, of the Society for the Study of Christian Ethics and of the Catholic Theological Association of Great Britain offered helpful comment. Geoffrey Nuttall made characteristically incisive suggestions. Jim Gibbs was central in the genesis of chapter 9. Without the ample and generous editorial help of David Parker and John Stokes there would hardly have been a book.

Peggy Fletcher, helped by her husband Bill, patiently and skilfully typed many drafts. David Columba and Tom Fallon showed their trust in the venture by kindly giving me house and study room respectively during a difficult intermediate stage. I am also grateful to two editors, John McDade of *The Month* and Anthony Dyson of *Modern Churchman*, for permission to reproduce here portions of articles of mine published in those journals.

The book is without footnotes, but an annotated bibliography at the end includes details of works mentioned in the text and of others which have had a significant influence.

Part One

1

Terror and Promise

Tar-blackened weather-scarred hut on bleak sea's edge epitom-ised the harshness and the terror of it. Why were we driving along this road? Where were we going? Whatever the answers we were travelling very fast, this haste also connecting with the terror. But what was the terror, given that we had a seemingly secure destination all prepared?

It was the war, about to break out. The birth of my mother's fourth child was very near, the three others of us being still very young. My father was staying in town, while insisting on our immediate evacuation into the country. What was to become of us all, and of England, and . . . ? All this and much more was the terror, though at the age of four I didn't know it. I only knew the terror.

Northumbrian farmers' and fishermen's children became our friends. While Hitler still did not come, official evacuees arrived from the inner cities, and departed, having told us things about sex we had not heard elsewhere. At the village school we were allowed to pick fruit in the headmistress's garden. The fat boy was bullied and taunted just like in the story-books, his back against the wall in the break-time. Encouraged by the mystical headmistress we chose books to read from the strange attic.

My father, a gracious but reserved weekend visitor bearing comics, took us on long walks round the bay to the enchanted headland ruin. On highly ritualised New Year's Eve the fisher-men, normally sober, suddenly filled our box-house with their released wildness before seeking entry elsewhere and everywhere, till later leaving it at that for another year. On Sundays we walked across fields to set up altar in the Craster Arms, which smelt strongly of Saturday night's beer. Here the priest from Ellingham said Mass, except once when no Mass could be said because he had forgotten to bring the right kind of bread.

At remote Ellingham itself in the chapel of the Haggerstons, the mantillaed dowager in attendance, I was confirmed prematurely, because the war made it in my mother's mind very uncertain when the Bishop would be able to come again. All I knew afterwards, with absolute assurance, was that something of tremendous importance had happened to me entirely to my surprise, for the preparation had been formal, lifeless and not without anxiety, while earlier sacramental experience had been unhappy.

And it was good. And all the while beach-sand silted around the concrete blocks, among the barbed wire, over the ancient cars plonked here and there to obstruct the foreshore against invaders, and into the dune dug-outs which became our hideouts.

But the terror, having been propagated, had taken root all unawares. It doesn't require the rampant paranoia of a Robespierre or Stalin to spread terror. There is always fertile ground for it long before we have much of a conscious say in our destiny, and it is then a question of what gets interiorised: its reign, I mean. So in Beadnell long ago this nameless, numbing terror lodged in me alongside cormorants, extensions of black cliffs against the sky, and those Northumbrian fishing-boats called cobles serene with lobster-creels.

Finally, as if all at once to confirm the terror in apocalyptic sign and to hold me in continued thrall, came the sky-filling nightmare of hell-coloured smoke-pall belched from a huge British oil-ship, bombed when Russia-bound, exploding to high heaven one mile offshore before my fixated gaze.

Another memory, not in contradiction of that dread doom-cloud but having a quite different tone and texture, is equally insistent. The names of two cobles spring to mind: Golden Gate and Sweet Promise. The first evoked a world, a future, in almost frightening contrast with anything I then knew – world of bright colours quite different from present pastel shades. Golden Gate. Some sort of transformation-scene. I pondered the name, but it would not yield its secret. Yet there was already in that name, painted on the hulk of a decaying coble, an insistence of mysterious invitation.

The appeal of the second boat's name, Sweet Promise, was and remains both gentler and more insistent; and this boat was still in business. Sweet Promise. A name transmuted on the fine, clear day they brought the airman back from the sea, he having dropped like a stone from his burning plane. I did not know till then that cobles could move so fast. This was a clean, terrible

4

swiftness. The grown-ups stood in a particular sort of silence at the sea's edge as the improvised tarpaulined stretcher was carried up the shingle.

It was the Sweet Promise, not the more worthily named Endeavour, which had thus urgently cast off her moorings to make like an arrow from the tiny harbour to a precise point in the sea. The boat was unbelievably swift, the man already dead, the promise not denied. The moment, like the name, recurs as a delicate assurance resisting all contradiction: Sweet Promise.

The promise is, or contains, an invitation. It is compelling only in the sense that something of almost unbearable beauty is compelling. Once seen, there is no way back without major loss, the desolation of a gift spurned and a chance missed. The promise and the invitation are not simply outside ourselves; they *are* ourselves, they touch us into life, into the one choice worth making. Not generated by us, mysteriously other than us; yet this living word is our homecoming. Love of God, love of self and love of one another are indivisible.

The shift in the last paragraph from story-line to theology may seem abrupt and even arbitrary. I make no apology for it, while readily acknowledging that my experience did not at the time find any theological words. Indeed as far as I can recall it found no words at all until very much later, when it became possible and desirable to tell this childhood tale, and thus to interpret it.

This revelation of created reality as a dialectic of terror and promise implied that if either was to cut deep enough the other would prove to be not far away. It was not in reason's gift to deduce which would have the final say, or even whether that was a proper question. But I retained a stubborn conviction that the promise, tested in the fire of new terrors, would be vindicated, though how and in what sort of world I could not imagine.

In my first book, *Death's Gift*, I sought to look from this vantage-point at the subject of resurrection and bereavement. Here I turn to consider a range of what seem to me fundamental strands of Christian living, trying to spell out some moral implications of the hope that is in us, that inexplicable gift born and nurtured in and out of terror. Central to the whole work is the conviction that what we like to think of as our sanity and our moral integrity must be put on the line if the gospel is to be taken seriously.

More specifically, while moral systems and systematic notions of human wholeness proliferate in flight from our mortality, Jesus in his own person and story dramatically reverses this flight. If we can see him as commentary on and commendation of this reversal we might perhaps be getting somewhere. We need to understand that Christian faith is not centrally about virtue or psychological integration.

It is not without interest, and certainly not without irony, that the current of biblical fundamentalism now running in most churches and the new papalist fundamentalism in the Roman Catholic church both find their security in the notion that the moral life is already decisively charted for us over a sufficiently wide field in Bible and Church. In other words a gospel, which in the searing story it unfolds presses beyond all systems and puts all securities in question, is being used to buttress conclusions reached on quite other grounds and now proclaimed oppressively in Jesus' name. There is little evidence to suggest that Jesus was all that interested in morality.

2

Inside Story

It is a hallowed Christian tradition that Jesus shows us how to live, or enables us to live in a certain way. This book as a whole attempts to show in what sense this claim can be sustained. To that end this chapter seeks to clear some ground by questioning the common assumption that the appropriate identification with Jesus proceeds by means of exposure to his morally uplifting teaching and the morally exemplary nature of his life and death. There is something curiously elusive about both the teaching and the example if we approach them in this expectation.

First, the example. Here we have a person who, having not infrequently avoided his enemies, sets his face towards Jerusalem at a moment of maximum excitement and danger in that city of conflict. He thus puts himself knowingly in line for the worst that can happen to him, and he does so for no clear cause, still less for one which could be called morally laudable. There seems to be something wanton about the Passion, not least because it can only leave his chosen ones in cruel disarray in a situation they do not understand.

True enough, we are told that he behaved thus in obedience to his Father's will. But this bare and totally uncorroborated claim is no help in establishing or drawing attention to any recognisable frame of reference which would make his behaviour morally commendable. This is not to deny that Jesus became convinced that his chosen course of suffering was the Father's will. But all sorts of people become convinced of all sorts of things and give all sorts of reasons, many of them less than convincing. The point here is that nobody else involved had any means of checking out the basis of Jesus' conviction. The claim to be enacting the Father's will, made in such circumstances, was unintelligible, all the evidence being that neither his friends nor his enemies could make anything of it.

From our point of view what moral principle or value-judgement or judicious anticipation of consequences could conceivably corroborate or make intelligible his sense that the Passion was not only something that must happen but something that would prove a blessing? I have in mind here the whole movement of Jesus' life towards Jerusalem, confrontation and death rather than any specific predictions of death and resurrection. It has always seemed to me very odd to assume, as most Christians do, that in the main thrust of the story of Jesus we have a straightforward moral ideal, or someone whom 'if only we were not so feeble' we would find readily imitable.

There is a comparable difficulty about Jesus as the greatest moral teacher. In the 1950s at Cambridge there was no little shock among some Christians at the reception into the Church of a certain professor. Addressing an undergraduate group he explained that he did not believe the stories about Jesus but that he was profoundly impressed by his moral teaching. In common with many others I was so fixated on what the professor claimed not to believe that the oddness of his positive assertion did not strike me! When I later came to teach Christian ethics this oddness struck home as I sought in the gospel texts elements of moral enlightenment. I found myself in a completely different world from that of the moralists of whatever hue. 'Let the dead bury their dead', 'If thine eye offend thee, pluck it out!'; the insistence on hating your relatives and much else in Jesus' teaching appeared not only impossible to reconcile with any moral system but subversive of such systems. Jesus seemed somehow not particularly interested in morality, but always to be starting from somewhere else.

It was not possible to leave the matter there. Although it was not clear to me what Jesus' starting-point was, he breathed a more bracing, joyful and life-enhancing air than the writings on morality which came my way. I could not help wondering what was at stake in the difference, and in particular why it was that so many people who thought they were expounding his teaching were doing something else.

Some light dawned with the realisation that whatever else Jesus' teaching might or might not be it was a commentary on his life and death. I saw that his teaching and his story could not be understood in separation from each other. His teaching was earthed in his story. He was not offering moral principles but some picture of what he himself was about, with the implication that we have it in us to be about the same thing, namely more abundant life. This by no means removed the sense of moral oddness for, as has already been said, Jesus' story is itself most odd from this angle. But at least I had now come to see that the strangeness of the life and that of the teaching were one and the same strangeness. This encouraged me to think more about the meaning for us of Jesus' story.

The question, 'Whose story are we living?' gives an emphasis significantly different from that of the usual form of discussion of moral questions. Are we living the gospel story, the story of Jesus? This question is proposed as an alternative to the moral absolutism which offers a check-list of what is right and wrong in every circumstance and equates orthodoxy with assent to this list. By contrast with allegiance to such abstract absolutes the question proposed might at first glance appear a soft option; but as the central character in the story is a man who offered himself to be crucified and in so doing alienated or baffled everyone with whom he had dealings, from Peter to Pilate, it can hardly be denied that to live this story involves a rigour all its own.

But what could it possibly mean to live the story of Jesus? Another form of this question is to ask what difference the story of Jesus actually makes now. Is it possible to establish any effective link between his story and ourselves? It has taken me a long time to recognise that these nagging questions are misplaced, for they assume that the story of Jesus is one thing and our story another. If, as I now suggest, it is all one story, with Jesus' teaching indivisibly a commentary on his life and ours, or on his story as ours, it follows that the difference he makes can only be discovered in the further living of the one story, for there is no vantage-point available outside it.

More specifically the death of Jesus, which is clearly the fulcrum of the tale as its first tellers recounted it, sets up an irreversible trauma in humanity. There is no way back from this death, no way of bypassing it, and no way of standing outside it. It is not that this death has consequences, nor that this death has made a difference: it is rather the key to our becoming. Only when the story of humanity is complete will we who make up in our own bodies what is lacking in the sufferings of Christ be able to say with any authority what the outcome is. And by then there will be no need to announce it, for everyone will know!

In arguing that we are on the inside of the story and therefore able to seek its fuller meaning only by living it out from within, I am claiming that we have a creative contribution to make. In our becoming there is the possibility of further chapters in the story. We are not, and are not called to be, mere replicas of Jesus. A human world peopled by such cardboard copies would be a nightmare. What then of the emphasis found in the Johannine and Pauline writings on the closest possible identification with Jesus? This seems to me to be secured in the appropriate way by insistence on the unity of the story, so that to be one with Christ or to be in Christ is to be living my own life to the full in the light of and under the power of Jesus' death.

This book commends the notion that in his Spirit, released in his death and now his gift to us, it is possible and desirable to allow the freest interaction between Jesus' story as we have it, our own unfolding story and the contributions of others in this and every age to the human story. It is possible and desirable to give the different strands space to illuminate and reinterpret one another, so that the story is always being taken further. One implication is that we can allow Jesus' story to interpret us in all our possibilities to ourselves. It has been hinted earlier that to cast Jesus as ideal and exemplar, and to understand his teaching in such a way, is to superimpose on the story told in our gospels a different and quite incompatible picture. Yet such a picture persists as testimony not to Jesus but to the craving for a larger-than-life hero who, enshrining all goodness in himself, will somehow do the whole thing for us and so assuage our terror. It is a supreme irony that such an image should be so persistently projected on to Jesus, who by getting himself crucified in the way he did might be thought to have gone out of his way to render such idealisation incredible.

Once such a projection has taken root it tends to be resistant to anything that might threaten it. Hence for instance the rage and panic with which many Christians responded to Martin Scorsese's film about Jesus before they had seen it. There was no need to see it before condemning it, because it was obvious that the film called in question the Jesus of the projection. There is an exact parallel in the burning of Salman Rushdie's novel, which refers to Mohammed, by people who are thought not to have read it. The response in both cases is understandable once the starting-point is understood.

The notion of Jesus' teaching as a commentary on the one human story rather than a collection of commands and aspirations needs further emphasis. He is constantly drawing attention to what actually happens, as in 'Judge not, that you be not judged'. Here the negative judgement I make on another's behaviour or attitude is recognised for what it is, a severe condemnation of myself. It is not that if I continue to condemn others I shall at some future date find myself condemned by others or by God. There is no need for such a condemnation even if it were appropriate, for I have already condemned myself. The saying is a brilliantly incisive way of saying that the habit of negative criticism, whatever it may or may not do to those criticised, paints the critic into a corner or confirms him or her in an anti-life posture. It is my distorted perception, not any divine decree, that judges thus. So I am encouraged by the saying to stop doing this destructive thing *to myself*. I am invited to observe in myself the full working of the dynamic of judgement and to believe that it can be transcended.

Sayings of this kind, then, influence us at a different level from what is ordinarily thought of as moral teaching. They draw attention to what, once awakened, we can see to be happening and capable of happening in our lives. They constitute an invitation into life, as does the story of Jesus which they illuminate. But the teaching and the story can invite us into fuller life only if severed from moralistic overtones. We cannot first reach a conclusion as to the moral difference Jesus makes and then commit ourselves to following him. It is only from within the continuing story that any worthwhile bearings on his significance are available, and they declare themselves only as our own becoming proceeds.

This conviction of an underlying unity in the whole story of human becoming can give an overwhelming sense of the closest possible identification with Jesus, as we seek to make more sense in our own living of his dying in and for humankind. To see it this way is to find warrant for reclaiming a creative responsibility for ourselves which allegiance to the fantasy of Jesus as moral exemplar and definitive moral teacher has enabled us to abdicate. This fantasy holds us in childish subservience rather than promoting that childlike openness commended and promoted by the gospel.

The next chapter involves an abrupt but temporary change of gear in order to illustrate this theme. It draws attention to the fact that it was the madness and suicide of someone who had become a tremendous inspiration and security to me which opened me up, indivisibly to myself and to the gospel as a living word. This awakening reactivated to remarkable creative effect the terror and promise rooted in childhood but in abeyance in the interim. Readers who cannot cope with poetry of any length would be wise to move straight to chapter 4.

3

There is a Balm: 23rd July 1964

Peter Luke Suart, monk of Downside Abbey in Somerset, took his own life on this date. As the onset of his disintegration reached crisis I, in those days a junior monk and completely under his influence, was put by the powers that be to supervise him overnight. Those hours had their fill of tense horror. It was when I left him that he took his life.

In all that happened then, as in the years of his death's contentious prelude and aftermath amongst us, life for me was changed and charged – or perhaps it began. This persistently problematic world, flecked with nightmare, would insist on becoming a radiant dwelling-place.

Nowadays a freelance writer and occasional speaker on theological themes, I live in the Handsworth area of Birmingham. This poem was written here in 1989.

I

New heaven,
New earth,
One world of wonder.
He saw it happening –
Or thought he did.
'Look where it got him!' they said.
Suicide or crucifixion:
Dire either way,
Not much in the difference.
That's what happens
If you are unwise or arrogant or deluded enough
To continue to insist
That you see
Something that makes all the difference.
Nowhere to go,

Nothing to be done
In all this universe
Commensurate with what you have seen.
No way back either
To what now seem children's games
And tutelage perpetuated
In God's name.

II

You saw something –
Perhaps the Kingdom –
Only to end up screaming.
What have I done?
Why am I forsaken?
Where is my place?
Where can I be any longer
In such a universe?
No ground,
No holding-ground,
Ground shifting,
Shifting sands,
Limbo alone,
Sheer sheol shallow shadow-land,
Vortex,
Inward spiral
After such high ecstasy
Of seeing.

III

Lord, have mercy:
Nurturer,
More than mind-mender,
Transfiguration;
You our utterly unmagical
Sure earthing,
Whose blood was poured out
With water,
POUR OIL HERE.
I mean, on Old Mendip's edge –
(that's where the action was,
but I saw no blood on the tarmac

that gleaming morning;
his injuries, the autopsy said,
being internal:
untouchable, we might be tempted
to say) –
And in this Handsworth
Incongruously juxtaposed
Twenty-five years on
For your purposes,
Day-star
And sear night's irradiation,
Lord of all hopefulness.

IV

Neither to Gilead
Nor to Aaron's beard
Is this promised balm confined.
POUR OIL HERE, EVEN HERE, FOR GLADNESS.
Domine, Dominus noster,
How wonderful is your name
In all the depths and heights,
In every length and breadth
Of this universe;
In each fragile particular
Of this becoming.

Part Two

4

Jesus and Morals

The awakening to the self whose true identity is in God, beyond all ego-formation, makes the teaching of Jesus, and especially his most abrupt and wild sayings, intelligible for the first time. Otherwise we have to find ways either of distancing these sayings or of turning them into a morality, which is to domesticate them. The books are full of desperate expedients for making the sayings either forgettable or bearable.

In matters of morality we tend to think in terms of commands – 'Do this!', prohibitions – 'Don't do that!', and aspirations – 'It would be wonderful if we could turn the other cheek, or go the second mile'. The category of aspiration or pious hope is a device for accommodating those emphases we are unable to ignore but which it seems hopelessly unrealistic to suppose we can implement! If we try to put Jesus into these categories some interesting but disconcerting results emerge. Let's take each category in turn.

The notion of a *command to love* is a very difficult one, even perhaps a contradiction in terms. In what sense if any is love something that can be commanded, especially in this context where Jesus goes on to speak of the gift of the Spirit? Could it be that in using the language of commandment he is struggling with the difficulty we have in thinking of morality in any other terms? Perhaps what he is really saying is something like this: 'If you will insist on thinking in terms of commands, all I have to say to you is, "Love one another!"' There could even be a note of irony in his usage here, for we can't love with clenched teeth however hard we try.

What is new is the addition of the phrase 'as I have loved you' to the well-known command to love. At stake is an identification with Jesus, a being identified with him, not merely passively but in a way which enables the disciples to live in his Spirit.

19

Another way of putting this is to say that this commandment is new because it belongs to and inaugurates the 'new age'. It proclaims a newly realised possibility.

Once this identification occupies the foreground the 'command to love' looks very different. It becomes much more an assurance than a command: you will find yourselves able to love as I have loved you. What is constitutive of the love that is at stake is the Spirit's gift of continuing identification with Jesus. The identification and the loving are indivisible. This is a momentous matter, for in this promise and this assurance humanity begins to enter into what has been recently and boldly called 'emotional equality with God'. At this point the notion of moral living as predominantly a matter of commands breaks down.

The point can be corroborated by trying to think of other sayings attributed to Jesus as if they were straightforward moral commands. Think of his remarks about hating your relatives, about plucking out your eye, about giving away all that you own, about not giving absolute priority to family funerals. These sayings are discussed elsewhere in this book. The point being suggested here is that we need a category other than moral command if we are to make any sense of them; and the notion of identification with Jesus under the sway of the Spirit opens up perspectives on his life and ours startlingly different from what is normally meant by morality.

The second of the categories mentioned at the beginning of this chapter is *prohibitions*, for many people the very stuff of morality. Here again Jesus is often taken to be toughening up the law, notably when he speaks about anger and about lustful thoughts. But these remarks are made in a setting where the detail of the law was sometimes presented as all-important. What Jesus seems to be saying is, 'If you must think in that way then at least do so consistently and across the board. If, for instance, you are hell-bent on draconian measures against the adulterer why not show comparable severity to the would-be adulterer? And if you are clear that it is wrong to kill one another, then at least be aware of the killing force of harboured anger. You must follow your logic through to the bitter end.' This becomes fully explicit when he says about the woman taken in adultery, 'Let he who is without sin amongst you cast the first stone.'

In summary I should want to say that just as many of Jesus' sayings, though couched in the form of commands, turn out on closer examination to be something else, so it is with sayings which at first glance look like prohibitions. The irony is that in what seem to be prohibitions he is commending an anti-prohibitionist mentality, because he sees the state of mind that is habitually identified with prohibition as repressive rather than life-enhancing. This is not to say that Jesus is commending what the prohibitionist condemns – to reach that conclusion is to fall into the trap of the prohibitionist's logic, which on its own terms is impeccable. Jesus rejects that logic, and in that sense is scandalously uninterested in morals.

What then of Jesus and *aspirations*, the third category in which we are inclined to consider morality? Commendations of turning the other cheek, not worrying about where your next meal is coming from, and imitating the lilies of the field have about them an edge and urgency quite foreign to the mental world of mere aspirations or pious hopes. Yet we can't suddenly start behaving like this just by thinking about it. From the point of view of moral guidance what use are these sayings? They can't be principles or rules, not least because they contradict other things Jesus said – and did. But to relegate them to the category of aspirations is to deprive them of all substance and immediacy.

Enough has been said to suggest that the attempt to categorise Jesus' teaching in terms of commands, prohibitions and aspirations reveals a puzzle, because the categories don't fit. It remains to be seen whether the *story* of Jesus will yield an obvious moral lesson. The familiar images – the man for others, the man who went about doing good, the one who laid down his life for his friends – suggest that the story may prove to be more promising ground than the teaching.

We are so used to the claims that these images make for Jesus that we perhaps don't notice something odd about them. Let's take the last first: 'Greater love than this no man hath, that he lay down his life for his friends.' Think of this from the disciples' point of view. What on earth was the use to them of this particular dying and death, cutting across their expectations and leaving them in a much more parlous plight than if they had never met Jesus? What we don't have here is the martyr syndrome in which the leader dies nobly for a good and truthful cause the nature of which is clear and agreed between him and his followers. Jesus' Passion fulfils none of these conditions: there is no nobility, and whatever was in Jesus' mind and heart the disciples clearly had no idea what was happening or why. In what sense if any could this be said to have been an act of love as far as they were concerned? It is only in passing through the ordeal of seeing it as no such thing that they are brought to a different and wholly original vantage-point.

We have to beware of allowing pious habits of mind to reduce this mystery, and particularly its aspect of ordeal, to manageable proportions and therefore to distort it. If the Passion is not readily understandable, then it is not straightforwardly capable of imitation in a moral sense. This is not to deny that we may find ourselves drawn by the Spirit into a similar course. That is a quite different matter from the conscious imitation of someone whose virtue we admire.

What then of the 'man for others', the man who 'went about doing good'? It is true that there are stories of healing, of deliverance, of feeding, of forgiving, of raising from the dead. But Jesus was by no means always available to others. He sometimes avoided situations where he knew that expectations of blessing would crowd in upon him. At other times he confounded expectation in the most brutal manner, as when he refused to speak to his own family when they were desperately concerned about him. Similarly he sometimes answered expectation in such a disturbing way that people were frightened, as in the story of the demoniac and the Gadarene swine. At the conclusion of this episode the local people who witnessed what happened 'begged him to leave their district'. In the case of healing it is said that 'power went out from him and healed them all'. And, in connection with that, what was going on when the woman with an issue of blood touched the hem of his garment? The picture here is more one of psychic forces on the loose in a hysterical situation than of the conscious and measured dispensation of appropriate healing. None of this is what we normally mean by 'doing good', which is being kind to people according to our lights.

Again, once he had 'set his face towards Jerusalem' it becomes clear that in his mind at least the range of 'man for others' activities, which for a time had loomed so large, are not at the centre of the story. There is a deeper destiny in play which has to do with his death. The two seemingly contradictory movements need to be held together, for each interprets the other. But, as it is the death which is subsequently proclaimed as the saving event, the 'man for others' aspect of the story needs to be interpreted in the light of Jesus' movement towards his death.

5

Clarifications

I am arguing that Jesus was characteristically unconcerned with ethics in any of the usual meanings of the word. This is to put negatively the conviction that in him new dimensions of moral consciousness begin to be explored.

Subsequent Christian thought and practice, unable or unwilling to sustain this freedom, have shown a strong tendency to relapse into a fearful and defensive moralism dealing in 'shoulds' and 'should nots' and, most dire of all, 'should haves' and 'shouldn't haves'. Situation ethics, in brave and well-intentioned reaction to a traditional morality which it sees as legalistic, ironically contrives to constrict love itself to the same straitjacket. Of all the possible forms of action or reaction in a given situation we are to opt for that which is most loving! Here in the very name of love the wearisome recitation of should and should not, should have and shouldn't have, is given a new lease of life.

Strange love indeed, akin to that of which King Lear sought to elicit a token from his youngest daughter Cordelia to show that she loved him more than her sisters. Thus the only daughter able truly to love was destroyed by Lear's insane insistence on having love quantified. Reduced to replying in her father's terms Cordelia could only say: 'I love your majesty / According to my bond; nor more nor less.' So much for the failure of situation ethics to recover the freedom of the gospel.

It has been said that guilt results from unlived life. It is possible to be so afraid of getting things wrong, a fear often instilled or strengthened by forms of morality, not least those taught in God's name, that our lives remain largely unlived, while guilt prevails. The rest of this chapter will suggest some of the notions of morality which in the interests of ending this reign of terror are, at least implicitly, undermined by the New

Testament. In parallel with these suggestions something will be said about the distinctive moral thrust of the gospel story.

Pride of place among common but suspect notions of morality must be given to the maintenance of ethical purity. The words put into the mouth of George Washington – 'Father, I cannot tell a lie!' – exemplify this beautifully. There is also the claim made by a monk obligated by his choice of monastic life to attend the early morning office of matins: 'I shall be able to say to my Maker that I attended matins whenever I could.'

Another commonplace notion is that of morality as setting or following an example. Yet for the story of Jesus example is not the point. When Roger Bannister ran the first four-minute mile his achievement was not that he set an example for others to imitate. Rather, by being the first person to run at this speed over this distance Bannister changed the possibilities.

Likewise with the life and death of Jesus. The possibilities for becoming ourselves, or if you prefer for the human adventure, were transformed for ever in and through these events. By himself living out to the end his own trust in changing possibilities Jesus put them on the map for everybody. This, I suggest, is what is meant by calling him the pioneer and perfecter of our faith. It was recently said that faith means 'trust in real awareness'. If this definition is acceptable it should not surprise us that it has tended to be the mystic rather than the moralist who has glimpsed the earth-shaking possibilities opened up by the story of Jesus.

To say that the possibilities are changed means that hitherto unsuspected resources can be seen to be in play. There is an awakening to new horizons of possibility. A vivid instance is the story of the martyrdom of Stephen in the Book of Acts (chs.6 and 7). The narrative proceeds in the light of the story of Jesus, yet there is nothing to suggest mere repetitive imitation.

When Stephen appeared before the council, in what was on any terms a deeply threatening situation, the members saw that his face was 'like the face of an angel'. No such radiance is even hinted at in any of the Passion narratives. Stephen then delivered an astonishingly composed and confident speech culminating in a ferocious verbal attack on his accusers. Anything less like Jesus' reported demeanour before Pilate and Herod would be hard to imagine. Yet as his accusers' reactive rage reached its height it was Jesus whom Stephen saw standing at the right hand of God, and as death approached it was Jesus to whom he commended his spirit. This is a tale of imitation, certainly, but only in the sense of identification in the Spirit. It is a matter of identification with the changed possibilities brought into play by Jesus' fate and now made freshly manifest in the particular circumstances and character of Stephen, significantly and substantially different from those of Jesus.

The point can be further illustrated by the sequel to Stephen's death – 'Those who were scattered went about preaching the word'; and to the work of Philip in particular the response was one of 'much joy' in the unlikely setting of a Samaritan city. These severely persecuted people, dramatically and brutally deprived of an outstanding member of their company, did not repine. They found themselves able to live in terms of the changed possibilities revealed by Jesus. The fact that they were nothing daunted was not the result of striving to imitate any moral heroism perceived in Jesus – no such note is struck at any point in the story – but the fruit of that identification with him in the Spirit which made possible *the free play of their particular gifts* in extremely adverse circumstances, along with a distinctive and contagious buoyancy when all seemed against them.

Central to the new perception which was already shaping their actions and reactions was a strong sense that weakness and powerlessness were by no means to be identified. Seeing in the explicit and total weakness of Jesus on the cross the hinge of humanity's story enabled them to transcend their own lack of any obvious moral wisdom or virtue. If Jesus on the cross manifested God's love for us at maximum intensity, the resultant power-play was quite other than anything they had formerly seen as power. But *it was power*, and precisely power in weakness. Stephen before his accusers was nothing if not empowered, and so in their defencelessness were the dispersed disciples after his stoning. There is a morality here, in the shape of trust in the gifts and the Giver. Example has little or no place in this dynamic, which operates through identification and therefore has no need of imitative striving after the heroic.

What then of standards and ideals? Are they not the very stuff of morality? Is it not the case that Jesus raises the moral standard, or represents the ideal? These rhetorical questions stake a claim against which subsequent chapters will have much to say and to imply. Here I ask outright whether people who advance this claim really mean it, and if so what it is that they mean. I cannot rid myself of the hunch that an *a priori* assumption is being made that raising the standard and representing the ideal is what Jesus *must have been about*. In other words it seems to be implied that if Jesus was all that subsequent doctrinal tradition has claimed for him (i.e. that he was God) a pre-eminent degree of ethical purity must have characterised him. To put the same point slightly differently, ethical purity is, in this view, of such decisive importance that only an absolutely exemplary degree of it could have rendered Jesus uniquely memorable.

The language of standards and ideals is oddly remote, impotent to stir, and much less to convert, the imagination. Such language functions in a grey and timeless world which does not resonate with the vibrancy of the gospel. The Jesus of the gospels comes through as too sharply in touch with the springs of life and too painfully and realistically aware of the death-dealing powers, as at once too earthed and too transcendent, to have had any truck with standards and ideals.

What reason is there to suppose that someone as immersed as Jesus in the multiple ambiguities of life would also have been a standard-bearer or ideal-promoter? To make appeal to any such flat and static reference-frame is to deny the radical changing of possibilities which is his accomplishment. How can being crucified be thought about in terms of a standard or ideal? Yet it is this element in the story that mysteriously provides the major focus of apostolic and early Christian hope. Identification with Jesus in his death, interpreted by his resurrection, is the key. From the moralist's point of view this is bizarre and even scandalous.

Take the theme of poverty as an example. Poverty is about letting go; it is not an ideal. Consider the story of Jesus and the rich young man. Jesus takes the man's question straight, but in face of his claim to have kept all the commandments takes the matter further. Jesus' response exposes the weak spot, or more accurately the untouchable factor in the man's life, his dependence on his 'great possessions'. Jesus exposes this without rebuke: indeed no words of his even mention this dependence. It is simply that the suggestion of giving it all up shows the young man where his heart is. The course the conversation takes brings the man up against *his own reality*. It is not at all a matter of Jesus laying down the law or presenting an ideal. He doesn't need to do so, nor is it to his purpose.

To say that Jesus is unconcerned with ideals is not to commend a soft option. Hard questions arise here. What is my defendedness? Or against what am I defending myself? What is the painful place not yet known and recognised, not yet anointed? This deep defence, unconscious of its aim, produces compulsive behaviour, that sustained guardedness which is so skilful, so habitual, so determined to reveal nothing. But this is to stress the negative. May it not rather be that I am in flight from the promise made manifest to me from the beginning? The promise without which life has no meaning and the future is a blank?

The meaning to be found is a meaning of God. That is to say, not just another meaning but the truth of who I am. To come to this meaning involves the abandonment or breakdown of many other meanings, the particularities here being vocational, as in the story of Jesus and the rich young man. We need to find out, or to be shown, what meaning we cling to. There has to be a clean break, and no break can be clean without being acknowledged. This reflection leads naturally into the final area of clarification to be touched on in this chapter, that of the divine will. Not only is there a strong tradition that morality is about doing the will of God: many public prayers ask that what we do shall be in accordance with that will. The existence of such prayers confirms the prevalence of the assumption that there is a probability of conflict between that will on the one hand and what we want to do or are most strongly inclined to do on the other.

To take such conflict for granted is to presuppose a divided self, for whom God's will and my own are pitted against each other. Yet if I, human being, am God's child, made out of love and for love, it must be the case that my deepest and truly integrating desire is for God. There can be no real conflict of interest between God's will and my true self, any more than there can be any contradiction between the true interests of one person and those of another. That deep habits of mind commonly impel us to think otherwise has to do with compulsive behaviour-patterns and distortions of perception which keep us, individually and corporately, apart from one another and out of touch with the living God.

The gospel, it seems to me, aims to awaken us from this false seeing and consequent constricted living. Its notion of the will of God is therefore not that of a pre-ordained plan or pattern at odds with what I want: that would be to construct the divine will in the image of the super-ego, as is commonly and oppressively done. What is at stake is rather the image of a God who seeks to awaken us to those most rich possibilities and creative desires buried in us, so that we may put to fullest use the gifts that are in us and promised to us in pursuit of these desirable possibilities.

The moral theologian Josef Fuchs makes the bold claim that self-realisation is an absolute demand on the human person. He is fond of quoting Aquinas to the effect that God is offended only through behaviour by which persons go against their own well-being. Fuchs regards self-realisation as an acceptable and helpful summary of the moral task. To give his claim more extended consideration here may help to elucidate what I am saying about morality in connection with the will of God and the true self.

To seek to be someone else would according to Fuchs be self-alienation. This is either a truism – unlikely from so acute a thinker – or it is an extremely telegraphic way of saying something that urgently needs to be said. Given that this author's great bugbear is a morality of divine commands and prohibitions, we may surmise that what he is warning against here is the morally slavish and stereotyped 'persona' such a morality is likely to produce. He seems to be saying that your morality has to be *you* in action from the very centre of your being and not from anywhere else. Fuchs is not denying either the inevitability or the desirability of being receptive to the influence of others, but he is insisting that there is something unique about the judgement personal conscience makes in any particular combination of circumstances. This judgement cannot be reduced to anything prescriptive, or to what some admired person says or does, without self-alienation.

Fuchs proceeds to clarify his claim with reference to Abraham Maslow, Carl Rogers and Erich Fromm, whom he takes to be the best-known proponents of theories of self-realisation. He holds that all three import some criterion of self-realisation other than the given self. In defining self-realisation in terms of psychological health and integration they are not really speaking of self-realisation at all, but only of a selective form of psychological fulfilment. By contrast, what is demanded is a positive self-realisation that proceeds from the significance of the given self.

Fuchs is absolutely explicit that his understanding of self-realisation implies continuous conversion from real and threatening self-alienation. He even goes so far as to say that self-realisation is the fruit of the Spirit in us, and holds that in the New Testament the language of 'bearing fruit' cuts deeper than 'observing the commandments'. A final clue to his meaning comes in his interpretation of the Sermon on the Mount, which he sees as giving instruction in authentic self-realisation. In particular Fuchs sees the first beatitude, about those who are poor, as including all the others, because it is about the truly poor, those who put their ultimate hope in God.

Two points emerge most strongly. One is that there is something unaccountable about the given self: it can't be accounted for or explained or defined by means of anything or anybody else. The second point is the God-connection: true self-realisation has to do with putting your ultimate hope in God. In both these ways Fuchs' notion of the self differs from that of Maslow, Rogers and Fromm, which he has criticised. The obvious thing to say about their picture is that it leaves the transcendent out of account. Fuchs, as we have seen, makes a more subtle criticism: but does not his own picture of self-realisation make exactly the same mistake? Is he not, like them, importing into his definition something extraneous and therefore limiting, namely the notion of God-dependence? Fuchs might well reply in the way of the theologian that this would depend on what is meant by God.

He posits a relationship and a form of dependence within that relationship which is intrinsic to authentic self-realisation. This relationship does not begin with self-awareness; it is there 'from the beginning', defining me, naming me, promising me a destiny. Self-realisation then depends upon the development of this relationship, which because of who God is cannot be at odds with my real interest and well-being. This is where the language of relationship reveals its inadequacy: we can't wholly avoid seeing the relationship with God on the analogy of one between two humans. This analogy becomes misleading, for God is the thought of me, God is my origin and destiny in a way no other human can be. To speak of self-realisation in terms of this relationship is therefore not to introduce some other and extraneous factor, but simply to make explicit the relationship without which there would be no self of which to speak. To think otherwise is to think of God as an object among objects or a being among beings, no doubt bigger and better than anything or anybody else but essentially limited and limiting, competitive with human self-interest rather than fostering human flourishing.

It is worth adding that the dynamic of human development in relation to the living God can only be a movement from immature to mature dependence, which must entail the fullest deployment of our human gifts and powers in helping to bring a more redeemed world into being. A precocious or one-sided spirituality would bypass that concern as being irrelevant to what really matters, namely the relationship with God. But this suggestion turns out to be another form of escape or denial, for it presupposes the possibility of a self related to God but to nothing and nobody else. This is a fantasy-self relating to a God who does not exist. The relationship with God is the defining and inclusive one, entailing our being in relationship indivisibly with everything and everybody. Otherwise it is idolatrous.

The will of God has to do with the calling and nurturing into full, vibrant life of people used to being at most half-alive, so that any awakening is liable to be drastic and the call for it shockingly at odds with what normally passes for morality. It is worth pondering for a moment on the number and range of those who, both in the Bible and in the subsequent history of the Church, abandoned or contradicted in the interests of God what many if not most people would have regarded as their responsibilities. Abraham's intention to kill Isaac and Jesus' exhortation to pluck out your offending eye are merely the most spectacular chapter-headings in that story, which is of course still unfinished.

6

Wishful Thinking

Two widespread opinions about Christianity and morality puzzle me. One is that Jesus offers distinctive moral teaching clearly superior to what is available elsewhere. The other is that he makes more explicit and comprehensive that morality which all right-minded people already in principle accept. The first opinion, often voiced as the conviction that secularised Western civilisation still owes a great deal to something called Christian morality, assumes that the gospel has a distinctive moral content. The second opinion assumes a broad moral consensus, which the gospel is seen as confirming. This opinion is held by those Christian moralists who subscribe to some theory of natural law, which revelation is seen as complementing.

Both these viewpoints take it for granted that Jesus was deeply interested in and concerned about morality. Even a thinker as iconoclastic about the Christian past as Don Cupitt does not question this premise, while strongly implying that all that has subsequently come to be called Christian ethics bears little or no relation to what Jesus was about. It is not enough to start as Cupitt does from the assumption that while Jesus commended a certain kind of ethics the Church has by and large promoted quite another kind.

In other chapters I seek to show that the thrust of Jesus' life and teaching was at most oblique to anything that could reasonably be called morality and not infrequently subversive of it. The prior question now arises: if it is clear that Jesus was not really interested in morality, why does it continue to be a major preoccupation within the Church, generating a compulsion to ascribe to Jesus a strong moral concern belied by the evidence? Both the opinions with which this chapter began reflect, I suggest, this compulsion. The view that Jesus offers distinctive and superior moral teaching, and the notion that he confirms and expands the highest agreed moral wisdom, are different forms of the attempt to say the best we can of him in terms of the *prior* assumption that morality is all-important. This assumption is being allowed to dictate the interpretation of Jesus.

The picture which then emerges helps to tame the terror of life by providing an idealised focus of our own morality: here is someone who in his teaching as in his life consistently and wholeheartedly represents the moral standard, who in so doing reassures us that our moral ideal is not in vain. This is a projection of the same kind as that which insists without substantial evidence on the exemplary sanctity, wisdom and virtuousness of some particular church dignitary. When an exalted religious leader, the Pope for instance, says something stupid or neurotic or merely silly there is among some a willing suspension of their critical faculties, with the result that a statement which is intrinsically worthless or even perverse is treated with inappropriate reverence, healthy discourse being thus inhibited.

There has to be someone who embodies our moral universe if we are to continue to feel secure. This sort of projection therefore tends to persist in the face of counter-indications about the person upon whom the projection is made, because it is not about the reality of that person. It cannot be, for its function is to protect me against the pain of living in the real world where I would have to take responsibility. In placing all moral wisdom and virtue in a particular person or persons the projection takes the edge off the search for meaning and purpose in our common life, a search in which, in reality, nobody else can play my part. Whether the particular person happens to be the Pope or Archbishop Tutu or Jesus doesn't make any substantial difference: the escape-process in play is the same. The idea that one person or group can be the repository of absolute goodness, or can be wise on their own, is an immaturity which if not outgrown lends itself to idolatry. The continuing power of such projection in Christian circles is shown by the common capacity to ignore Jesus' warning: 'Why do you call me good? No one is good but God alone.'

It is instructive to anatomise further the attitude under consideration. It could be characterised as a 'thin end of the wedge' approach: not so much a passionate conviction that moral standards are of decisive importance as a sort of panic in the face of the alternative. The unspoken and perhaps unconscious premise seems to be that the alternative to a high profile for morality is anarchy and chaos. Fear of the disintegration and dissolution of individuals, and probably more importantly of communities, insists that morality reigns supreme.

Kierkegaard saw perhaps more clearly than anybody that if morality is to be given such predominance then ethics has become God. Hence his commendation of the 'teleological suspension of ethics' in the name of faith. Ethics must give way if the mysterious purposes of the living God are to be attained. It is significant from the point of view proposed in this book that Kierkegaard's suggestion has not found much favour with subsequent Christian moralists.

Despite Kierkegaard, the observable fragility of even the highest achievements of human civilisation might seem to corroborate the importance of morality. Unfortunately this consideration begs the question whether morality has power of itself to sustain civilisation, or whether it is not merely part of the waxing and waning of particular cultures. When people so readily attribute the alleged decay of our society to a decline in moral standards, are they not unwarrantably attributing to morality a most remarkable power? What evidence is there or could there be that morality is in a position to make or mar a civilisation?

It is hard to avoid the conclusion that a heavy investment in morality is really about something rather less reputable, namely the attempt at social control, the attempt to be in control of life and death. It has been wisely observed that currently fashionable theories of moral development are really about social adjustment. The ability to give increasingly principled reasons for a particular hypothetical course of action is taken to indicate that the person concerned is entering a high stage of moral development. In reality such a person is merely manifesting a capacity for articulate social conformity. If this is how moral development is defined it is being used as an instrument of social control.

To return to Jesus, it is hardly an accident that he reserved his most bitter invective and his most sustained argumentation for those who claimed to have everything sewn up, who assumed that their tradition had an answer to every question and a solution to every problem. He accuses such people of refusing the new life which is on offer for themselves and preventing others who desire it from entering into it. They are even described as 'children of hell'. While those whom he thus stigmatised lived in a very different age and culture from neo-scholastic casuists on the one hand and followers of Kant on the other, a similar claim is being made in all three cases – not to speak of those Christians who appeal to something called 'biblical morality'. In their claim to comprehensive moral certainty such approaches are oppressive and life-denying, in the first instance to their adherents and in consequence to those over whom they have influence.

That having been said, the point is not to attack particular groups or schools of thought, but rather to draw attention to the craving that is in us all for an all-embracing moral system to assuage our anxiety. It is only when the fruits of this craving are recognised as the destructive flight from reality that they really are, that the gospel can begin to come into its own. Then the world of the child and the sight of the lilies of the field can begin to work their way in us.

Despite what has so far been said I should not want to argue that the phenomenon of projection is always destructive. It necessarily plays a considerable part in our formative years, for without it we should be dangerously unprotected. But the moment comes when all such projections have to be withdrawn if we are to live our own lives to the full. I suggest that the call to be identified with Jesus is in its negative aspect an insistence that projections, like morality, are not transforming. One implication of this is that Jesus refuses to offer a morality, whether distinctively different from other moralities or confirmatory of 'what all good men and women think'. To offer a morality would be a distraction from his vocation to life through death, into which he calls us. To suppose otherwise is wishful thinking.

It is worth recapitulating in summary form the two central points of this chapter. One is the claim that there is an endemic human craving for a moral system, the other the observation that many people tend to project onto Jesus as the validating exemplar of such a system. Such a projection sees Jesus as primarily a teacher of morality. My argument is that this focus hopelessly obfuscates our awareness of and capacity for identification with the story of his life and death.

7

Imitation?

With the coming of Jesus, it is commonly assumed among Christians, something new in kind enters upon the human scene *from the outside*, wherever that is supposed to be. With his coming he brings a morality quite other than anything that has gone before. To think on these lines is to divorce the story of Jesus from the historical situation which produced him and of which he is the furtherance. What then comes into play is not a creative discontinuity but a false supernaturalism, which claims that he set standards hitherto unheard of and quite unattainable by human effort, while at the same time supplying to those who follow him the grace they need.

By contrast the argument of this book is that the life, death and resurrection of Jesus, taken together with his teaching, give access from within to new and open horizons in the one unfolding story of humanity or, more fully, of God-with-us. What Jesus illuminates and fosters is what is already there, or more accurately what is already in process of becoming. He is himself the fruit of that process, to which in his turn he contributes decisively in making accessible to us the uplands of the Spirit.

It is therefore not where he comes from but where his life and death take the human adventure that is crucial. What matters is where we are enabled to get to in our own living and dying in this world by way of identification with his death. Of course the resurrection, by elevating Jesus' death to the status of a mystery, raises questions about his origin in a peculiarly intense form. But the heady speculations that easily result from such questions must not be allowed to diminish or distort either his humanity or our potential solidarity with him in writing new chapters of the one story in our own lives now.

The difference is between a despairing or heroically sacrificial imitation of an imagined all-virtuous superperson, such imitation being fuelled by a strange commodity called grace, and on the

other hand creative identification with one who, by putting himself at risk in the exploration of new ground to the end, enables
us in our own time and way to pioneer possibilities hitherto
unrealised. This is strongly hinted at in the New Testament
conviction that the kingdom of heaven is in our hands. I am
seeking to draw attention to the difference betweeen the attempt
to be a moral replica of Jesus and the adventure of seeking to
live your own life to the limit in the light of his story, supported
by those who are caught up in the same task.

It could reasonably be objected that we all need models of
virtue or excellence, and that Jesus is the best possible model. I
agree not only that we need models but that we find them and
imitate them long before we have even thought about it. The
most obvious example is the influence of parents on children,
who imitate parental grace and sin from the beginning. Later a
teacher or a friend becomes a model for imitation, and so it goes
on. Such uncalculated imitation proceeds in our lives in a myriad
ways, some very obvious and some markedly less so, for better
and for worse. But this habitual and largely unconscious form
of imitation is not what the following of Jesus is about.

This following entails an identification which, instead of tend-
ing to replicate in detail the behaviour of the one imitated, leads
instead to the living of my own life in the spirit in which Jesus
lived his. Thus the letter to the Hebrews claims that because of
what happened to Jesus we have come to a point where everyone
is a 'first-born son' and a citizen of heaven. In the context of
what is claimed elsewhere for Jesus as the first-born this is a
bold claim indeed. But that very boldness, along with the fact
that the present tense is used, makes the point. We are gifted to
pursue our respective and distinctive journeys not in slavish
subordination to him and his example but in conscious continuity with his journey and achievement and in full solidarity
with him.

The word 'gift' can hardly be overstressed here. We can't
think ourselves into such continuity and solidarity, but at blessed
moments we can recognise that it is in this way that we are
being schooled at our very core; or at least that we are being
called so to live and are promised not only that we can so live
but that our fulfilment lies in doing so. This has a great deal to
do with the dissolution, often seemingly accidental and even
arbitrary, of longstanding securities.

There is no hint here of a morality from another and purely

supernatural world. What I am speaking of has to do with the earthing of us, just as it has to do with our coming into touch with the transcendent flame that burns at the very heart of this universe. Far from being a superman who can only be understood as coming from elsewhere bringing a supremely exalted moral message, Jesus epitomises human living at maximum intensity, human living pressed beyond its hitherto assumed limits. Becoming fully human is the project he presses passionately towards its consummation, and in so doing serves all those who take this project seriously, no less those who went before him than those who come after. Recall the haunting words of the Jesus of the fourth gospel: 'Your Father Abraham rejoiced that he was to see my day; he saw it and was glad.'

I sometimes have a sense that what Jesus opened up in pursuit of this goal was so staggeringly ambitious on our behalf that we are still in part paralysed rather than empowered by the degree of exposure and risk involved. Hence, perhaps, regressive forms of slavish imitation, which keep the real opportunity and task at a distance. In the meantime the identification with him which is on offer finds its sign in the Eucharist, in which we 'celebrate the Lord's death until he comes.' Have we begun to glimpse what this might mean for our own living and dying, and for the destiny of humanity?

Part Three

8

'If Your Eye Offends You . . .'

Central to this book is the claim that any serious and sustained attempt to find the meaning of Christian faith must put at risk our sanity and our moral integrity. However disturbing this claim may be, the New Testament and the lives of very many saints hardly gainsay it, while contemporary psychological insight offers sharp corroboration, often unknowingly. There is also Shakespeare's King Lear, who will provide my most extended example.

At the start of the play King Lear in old age is presented as a man of enormous and uncriticised ego. He is about to divest himself of the responsibilities of his kingdom by dividing it between his three daughters. Before announcing the detail of the division which he has already decided upon he insists that each daughter must publicly voice her love for him, ostensibly that he may be sure which loves him most and reward her accordingly. Faced with this outrageous demand Goneril and Regan have no difficulty in uttering honeyed words which cost nothing. Cordelia, the youngest and the only daughter truly to love her father, is tongue-tied: 'What shall Cordelia do? Love, and be silent.'

Lear's trivialising and psychologically brutal game turns instantly sour with Cordelia's refusal to play, and his rage is ungovernable. Hitherto it has been possible for him to assume that those around him were at his beck and call, with the implication that they existed merely as extensions of his personality. Cordelia refuses to collude with this state of mind. The faithful Duke of Kent moves rapidly to her defence, telling the King he is mad to reject her:

> . . . be Kent unmannerly
> When Lear is mad. What wouldst thou do, old man?

Enraged now beyond measure, Lear summarily banishes the

man who has his interests at heart and confronts him with the truth. He is still riding high as the reigning monarch possessed of all his faculties.

It is only when he is reduced to nothing except a different and threadbare and self-confessed form of madness – 'My wits begin to turn' – that Lear's salvation takes shape. Against the onset of this madness he had already prayed:

> Oh let me not be mad:
> Not mad, sweet heaven.

In the event heaven graciously encourages his madness to find full scope, for nothing else could break open the armour which encased him. How else was this man to be brought beyond his absurd strategy and posturing into the truth of his own heart? In Lear a spurious sanity breaks down and loses its grip. He has to go mad to be brought to the truth of things, to acceptance and acknowledgement of responsibility, and to the capacity to give and receive love: 'I am a very foolish, fond old man.' In and through traumatic disintegration Lear's gaze clears. He begins to see straight for the first time. Edgar notes the paradox:

> Oh matter and impertinency mixed:
> Reason in madness.

In the same play the Duke of Gloucester is blinded. His enemies, whom he had thought to be his friends, pluck out his eyes. The Duke's sight plays the same role in the story as the King's sanity. Gloucester is subsequently in no doubt that he is in better case sightless than seeing. He voices this conviction with maximum economy of words to those who take pity on him for his blindness: 'I stumbled when I saw.' In this connection it is worth recalling that Saul of Tarsus was blinded, albeit temporarily, on the Damascus road, and the Lord to whom he in consequence gave his allegiance was the one who had earlier cried out: 'If your eye offends you, pluck it out.'

The hyperbolic form of this saying should not distract from the truth it seeks to show forth: the violence that needs in one way or another to be done to unregenerate ways of perception if there is to be hope. Lear is driven out of his worldly wits into a transparent madness which frees him from his egotistic prison-house, the vehicle of destruction. Gloucester is by unspeakably barbaric means released from a superficial and partial seeing which had made him evil's dupe.

The theme of a movement from crooked to straight seeing by way of blindness is rehearsed in a quite different and distinctive way in the fourth gospel. The story of the man born blind makes clear that not everything is what it seems in this business of seeing and being blind, any more than it is in the matter of sanity and madness. After the healing Jesus said, 'For judgement I came into this world, that those who do not see may see, and that those who see may become blind.' Hearing this some Pharisees, who had gone to great lengths not to believe that Jesus had healed this man, asked him, 'Are we also blind?' Jesus answered, 'If you were blind, you would have no guilt; but now that you say, "We see", your guilt remains.' Their deficiency is not at all their failure to see but their refusal or inability to become blind. Their insistence on seeing, everywhere and in all situations, betrays them. There are no short cuts, and becoming blind must precede seeing straight.

But is not Shakespeare's Lear altogether larger than life? Not so, once we begin to notice the day-to-day manipulations and power-plays which characterise so much in the routines of inter-personal and inter-group communication and which wreak havoc domestically and in the wider world, to our bewilderment and shame. 'All through history,' writes Ernest Becker, 'it is the "normal, average men" who, like locusts, have laid waste to the world in order to forget themselves.' He adds that while in any particular instance such a person 'may avoid the psychiatric clinic, . . . somebody around has to pay for it'.

Bonhoeffer made a suggestion which converges with this. He claimed that the pharisee, far from being the blatantly hypocritical stereotype created by Christian prejudice, is that wholly admirable person who insists on seeing everything in terms of the knowledge of good and evil. The unlearning of such knowledge, Bonhoeffer argued, is necessary if Christian ethics is to get off the ground, for this knowledge is the barren fruit of humankind's alienation from our origin. I should want to make it explicit that this alienated or divided condition is the state in which the entire human race finds itself. It would therefore be a mistake to think of the pharisee as a person or cast of mind outside or over against ourselves.

Studies of Christian morality since Bonhoeffer rarely if ever recognise the wisdom of his commendation of the unlearning of the knowledge of good and evil as the prerequisite for Christian ethics. This suggests that the cast of mind he attributes to the pharisee is deeply entrenched, for Bonhoeffer is readily quoted on other topics. Perhaps this reticence connects with the fact that our thinking about morality has become accustomed to inattention to much that the gospels report Jesus as having said. Though very many within and outside the Church assume that he was a very great moral teacher, this conviction does not usually focus on the 'hard sayings'. I suggest that long-term exposure to these sayings without any increment of understanding has had a curiously distancing effect, so that the fictional Lear and Gloucester may even appear more credible than, 'If you eye offends you, pluck it out,' or Jesus' remarks to those pharisees after the blind man became able to see.

Bluntly, it is a question of whether or not we have noticed in ourselves and others the dynamics of the endemic human flight from reality. Or is it that, having glimpsed this terrifying process of attempted escape from our own becoming, we have repressed the memory and continue to live as if all is simply and sheerly well? If this latter is the case our mistake is to suppose that if this fiction is not sustained we shall subside into final despair. Wiser are the words of Etty Hillesum, written in a situation of very severe deprivation where grounds for hope might be thought to have been far to seek: 'Everywhere things are both very good and very bad at the same time.' She came to see that the two can live together, and that within the range of present consciousness neither simply disposes of the other. The terror and the promise do not cancel each other out.

A parallel point comes from Bonhoeffer:

> Shakespeare's characters walk in our midst. But the villain and the saint have little or nothing to do with systematic ethical studies. They emerge from primaeval depths and by their appearance they tear open the infernal or the divine abyss from which they come and enable us to see for a moment into mysteries of which we had never dreamed.

It must be emphasised that the villain and the saint – and are they different people? – are only ourselves writ large. They are what is being made of the humanity of us all, so that if we are out of touch with the 'primaeval depths' which are ours we are lost indeed. It is a severe mercy that brings us into touch with those depths and nurtures us there. For King Lear that mercy took shape in the loss of his wits, for the Duke of Gloucester in his blinding, and no doubt we should like to think that no such extremities will be asked of us. But if our faith means anything, the unlearning of whatever holds us back from the consummation will proceed in whatever way it can.

The surrender, that yielding up of attitudes and forms of behaviour assumed hitherto to be not only right but definitive, is always specific. It is therefore initially intelligible only in terms of the particulars of your journey and no other, yet it has about it a universal quality. That is why the gospels came to be written in witness to the story of Jesus, seen by way of redeemed memory as good news for humankind, that is to say as our story, still unfinished and even perhaps scarcely begun, but to be lived in faith, hope and love.

'If your sanity offends you, let go of it!' might epitomise what this chapter is trying to say. If holiness is too readily equated with particular images of wholeness or integration, this suggestion will be thought shocking. But I believe it to be wholly in the spirit of the 'hard sayings', which invite us into the real world where neither psychological wholeness nor moral integrity are at the centre, where there is only and always God. It is at best unwise to encourage someone, yourself or another, to pull themselves together at a moment when what he or she is being drawn to do is to fall apart.

I am arguing that the living God promotes or is involved in the disintegration of Lear. Lear is able to behave as if he is the absolute centre of the world. He then experiences *for himself* the necessary consequences in a world which isn't made like that. The story of Lear is about rebirth in truth and love. The workings of divine love are not tied to the proprieties of what we like to call civilised life. God takes us and the cosmos rather more seriously than that.

The vertiginous loss of security involved in this kind of madness can hardly be overstated and is very much to the point. When the securities of our time of formation, having served their turn, become monumental at the expense of new life in ourselves and others the shake-out from them can hardly be less than cataclysmic.

The declension of Lear into madness is a clearing of the plugs, this alone being sufficient to strip this man of his continuing pretension to dominate; for even his magnificent defiance in the storm is hardly free of posturing self-absorption. The disintegration of Lear is swift and terrible. Yet the outcome is that he becomes, in utter helplessness but with sureness of touch, a person at last. The making of Lear even reaches a point where he demonstrates an artless love so poignant as to be hardly bearable to the onlooker once it becomes clear that its chief object, Cordelia, is dead. Many have felt that this last twist is altogether too much, and for a long time the play was only performed with Shakespeare's unrelievedly tragic ending replaced by a 'happy' one. But this is to assume that Cordelia's death, swiftly followed by Lear's own, renders pointless or useless the change already wrought in Lear.

Jesus, 'having loved his own, loved them to the end'. This is exactly what Cordelia and Lear did, she consistently throughout and he authentically once he is readied for this love by his ordeal. If their love is adjudged pointless what are we to say of Jesus? The gratuitous nature of his love is horribly masked by the assumption commonly made that he really had the whole thing sown up – and in particular the structure of the Church mapped out and secured – before he left the scene. This error succeeds in making the resurrection the solution to a conundrum rather than a deepening and confirmation of the mystery of Jesus' life and death. Thus is the gospel story distorted out of recognition and the gratuitous love of Jesus left nowhere as the great plan of salvation clicks relentlessly into gear. King Lear and all that soon cease to be of interest in such a scenario!

9

'When the Son of Man Comes . . .'

An assumption common among scholars is that the very first years of Christian faith were characterised by a strong expectation that Jesus was about to come again, an expectation which waned as the years passed without any such occurrence. That such should have been the bedrock and universal conviction of the immediate post-resurrection years has always seemed to me odd. Had it been so, how could this movement have retained creative vitality after the disappointment? Too much would have had to be abandoned.

What was being posited seemed an eccentric state of mind which did not inspire confidence in the reliability of these first witnesses. If they thought Jesus would come again very soon, where did they suppose he was in the meantime? What sense could be made of the image of the company of believers as his body? Oddest of all, how could people so obviously certain of the present power of the risen Jesus and their own identification with him *also* think in terms of the second coming, which must presuppose a sense of absence? I was therefore grateful to come upon an alternative view which also enjoys some scholarly support.

This second opinion is that the first Christians did not have a strong expectation of the second coming. They had no need of it or desire for it because they already had an overwhelming sense of the presence and empowering of the risen Lord in the present. It was only as *this* conviction waned that preoccupation with the second coming began to obtrude. This picture is more readily intelligible: an initial confidence in Jesus' continuing presence and power becomes eroded by life's rough-and-tumble to a point where the second coming looms large in default of anything more centred and vibrant. An understandable loss of nerve and balance, succeeding upon the exuberant enthusiasm of the beginnings, generates a none-too-convincng appeal to the second coming.

It is tempting to take the second of these interpretations as alone authoritative, thus releasing us from any need to take the second coming seriously. It makes considerable sense to consider Christian origins in terms of a time of vibrant faith giving way to a period of shadowy apocalyptic fantasy in which the Lord's imminent return was a major element. If preoccupation with the second coming springs from a diminished awareness of the Lord's present empowering, the future image is likely to function as wishful thinking in compensation for present hopelessness. If this note of rather desperate fantasy is all that there has ever been to it the sooner we abandon the preoccupation the better.

There is a seductive simplicity in this suggestion that notions of the second coming are expendable when Christian living is at full throttle. By contrast I suggest that *both* insistence on the risen Lord's present empowering *and* stress on the second coming are attempts to answer a single question: how can we continue to live in the light of the shock of the death of Jesus? That was the question implicit in the beginnings of the Church. It is a question which refuses to go away and remains a source of inexhaustible creativity. What we are involved in is not simply an event in the past which had certain effects now available and transparent to the dispassionate observer. We are on the inside of the story, as I insisted in an earlier chapter. It is a story which is unfinished in that the shock-waves persist and have not yet been worked through.

We therefore cannot answer the question, 'What difference has the death of Jesus made to human flourishing?' What we can do is to declare this the wrong question. The questions that need to be put have to do with what we are making of this death, and how our involvement in it is contributing to the outcome.

Jesus said, 'When the Son of Man comes, will he find faith upon the earth?' I used to hear these words as a heavily moralising attempt to get us all to pull our socks up, in a tone which suggested we were unlikely to measure up to the required standard! Subsequently Jesus' words came to acquire a haunting resonance for me as a perception of the fragility of present faith: 'By the time this story reaches its conclusion will there be anything left?' It is an anguished question to which there is no reason to assume that Jesus knew the answer. It is more a matter of continuing to hope against seeming impossibility. The question puts the ball back in our court, in appeal rather than exhortation. Instead of Jesus being gloomy about the future we have him being electrifying about the present: 'Are you alive to what is happening? Is anyone alive to what is happening?'

Karl Rahner said somewhere that without the resurrection appearances and the formation of the new community there would have been no resurrection. That must be true unless we make of Jesus' resurrection an absolutely disparate event. In that case the resurrection is something which might and could have occurred anywhere at any time but just happened to happen, by divine decree of course, when and where it did. In reality the disciples were central and indeed indispensable to the event, not because they created it – in truth it creates them – but because there is never a disparate event. The context is always integral to the happening. This particular group of people with the particular form their involvement with Jesus had taken is integral to the event of his resurrection. Those of whom it is the making, initially and decisively for all that follows, are necessarily those at the very centre of the shock-waves caused by Jesus' death.

These people seem to have spent the rest of their lives speaking and acting in a remarkable variety of ways out of the shock. The resurrection is their story in both meanings of that phrase: it is the story they tell, but it is equally the story of them. To consider the resurrection as in any way separable from their state after Jesus' death is to reduce it to a disconnected phenomenon. The risen Lord came to his own bearing his wounds, and they became an enspirited community. That is the kind of thing the resurrection of Jesus is. It is only in and through such intense particularity that the claim emerges that he is humanity's salvation.

Likewise with all that follows. Identification with the risen Lord and expectation of his final coming, superficially exclusive of one another, are emergent strands in believers' response to the continuing shock of the loss of him. To categorise these convictions in this way is not to devalue them but to situate them in the setting in which they arise, and in so doing to render them both intelligible and mutually compatible. Once this is recognised the questions come back to us. How do we relate to the death of Jesus? Where are we in the trauma? What are we doing with it? If we are inclined to think that expectation of a second coming in the form we find it in the New Testament represents a flight from the reality of Jesus' death, what is our alternative? Where is our hope, given that there is no way back from this death and the world often seems wretchedly and even frighteningly unredeemed, if not impervious to redemption? If the question of our present hope is never seriously broached, our eucharistic celebration will be at best a mixture of pious nostalgia and fantasy. What meaning can there be in worship that fails to draw the participants into new awareness of and truthful response to the creative disequilibrium involved in and continuing to be provoked by this death?

Theories about the place the second coming had in the belief of the early communities are too tied to the assumption that it is possible to have only one response at a time to Jesus' death. I therefore suspect that both the very strong sense of Jesus' present empowering and a note of overwhelming anticipation, along with a very great deal else, were around from the start, though not pressed home always and everywhere with equal vigour. From this point of view it is a grave impoverishment to conclude that notions of the second coming are not quite reputable, theologically or spiritually. We need to recover a sharp sense of what is at stake in this area of expectation.

It is a question of how we see the world, and Jesus' relationship to it. Is it a world of discrete events – there was a death and there will be a second coming – or is it an about-to-come-to-an-end world, shown to be such by the death and resurrection of Jesus? If the former, we are offered a featureless plain between one critical moment and another. This will tend to make of morality a holding action, with the implication that change can only be a betrayal of known standards. If on the other hand we live in an about-to-come-to-an-end world everything is in the making, in travail with the trauma of this death which breaks open the encrusted earth and the hardened heart. This makes of morality something necessarily innovative. If we do not live on the knife-edge of hope in and through loss we are not yet awake to the gospel. Without such expectation the moral dimension of the gospel is invertebrate, and we would be wise to refuse to take it seriously.

If anything in the moral sphere is distinctive of Christianity it is not some ethical doctrine, superior or otherwise, but a living hope. This hope is the call and the gift of God in Christ Jesus, who by being lifted up is drawing all humankind to himself. Or is he? Is that what his death means? Is his Passion the final convulsion of a fractured universe in travail with its own true life? Is his death, interpreted by his resurrection, the coming to birth of the new world? Is the risen Jesus the first-born of many, and in principle of the human race, or not? Do we, or do we not, live in an about-to-come-to-an-end world? All these questions are really forms of the same question, addressed from faith to faith in connection with a specific hope. Hope, like faith, turns out to be a gift, not a possession. Our faith invites living in hope rather than by any ethical doctrine; for any such doctrine would involve some notion of the good life, whether for myself, for others or for all. All such notions live only by a systematic repression of awareness of personal and cosmic death.

It is dismaying that only in the debates about nuclear deterrence and ecological concern is there any serious attention within mainstream Christian thinking to the question of the end. Otherwise we leave theological preoccupation with this question to those we regard as on the fringe, and then ridicule the crudity of their apocalyptic. This suggests that we have far more confidence in our own ability to destroy the world than in God's power to bring the whole thing to a joyful consummation.

The way of Jesus is the way of life through death. In opening up this way he both brings the old world to an end and launches us into an about-to-come-to-an-end world. If the death of Jesus questions all human living and dying and declares the true thrust of all life in this world, the consequences for morality are devastating. Yet many Christians still think of morality in terms of a 'finger in the dyke' approach, as if there is so little ground for hope and celebration that the best we can do is to seek to block the flow of evil at some particular point, whether it be divorce, nuclear weapons, environmental pollution, social and economic injustice, abortion, or whatever. In face of the grimness of this approach it must be emphasised that Jesus' death means that the new world is truly born. This is not to say that all issues are already resolved, but that they are henceforth being resolved in a context where evil is on the defensive. Thus the world is always about to come to an end. That is the kind of world it is.

The preparation of the heavenly banquet proceeds in time, prompted by the urgency of God's love for everyone and sustained by the divine patience. But this theme loses all momentum if the options remain open for ever. As regards time and the expectation of the end the point is that *it takes as long as it takes* for the celebration to take over. The gospel is most insistent that the time of the end, whether in terms of an individual's life or of

51

the world, is not for human beings to know. Far from advocating indifference, our texts commend urgency in the present, as against the false humility which teaches that I am so small a creature and the present time so insignificant that I have no substantial part to play in the unfolding of the mystery.

Our opportunity, our responsibility to the future lies in helping to create one another's lives in the present. The moral task is total engagement with present reality. This engagement might be characterised as wakefulness, attentiveness, obedience in the full and freedom-inviting sense of that much-abused word. It would be ludicrous to deny that ethical doctrines have their uses, but disastrous to regard them as the heart of the matter of morality. Where that happens life lived through death is reduced to a set of ideals. Thus is the mystery, and in particular the coming of the end, denied; for the structures of relationship which produce such ideals are already passing away, and are in any case fragmentary and partial. To place our hope in them is to be idolatrous. Our living hope says, positively and expectantly, 'Here is no abiding city.' Otherwise we are bound to be ruled by distortions: for no ethical doctrine, however noble, can put us in touch with the one who is the very heart of all reality, the one who is both the pillar of cloud and the pillar of fire, whose purposes will be accomplished and whose mystery is inexhaustible, who can only be adored.

Listen to the cautionary tale by R. S. Thomas of Morgan the Minister in the Welsh hills:

> He never listened to the hills'
> Music calling to the hushed
> Music within; but let his mind
> Fester with brooding on the sly
> Infirmities of the hill people.
> The pus conspired with the old
> Infection lurking in his breast.

Morgan was destroyed by letting a narrowly moralistic preoccupation turn him off the encounter with the mystery.

In contrast stands Alfred of Wessex, glimpsed by G. K. Chesterton at his lowest point in the desperate struggle against the Danes:

> He saw wheels break and work run back
> And all things as they were;

> And his heart was orbed like victory
> And simple like despair.

Unlike his allies in the great battle Alfred came through to triumph:

> Because in the forest of all fears
> like a strange fresh gust from sea,
> Struck him that ancient innocence
> That is more than mastery.

Alfred is someone for whom all normal grounds for hope have gone. Precisely when he is without resource he is shown the ancient innocence 'that is more than mastery', quite other than the innocence of simply not knowing how dreadful things can be. It is a gift, and an invitation to live in lively expectation. Ethical doctrines, concerned as they are with mastery, know nothing of this blessed assurance.

10

'Why Do You Call Me Good?'

A strand of contemporary scripture scholarship pursues the question of why Jesus was put to death. Intriguing hypotheses have emerged, but the trouble with the whole exercise from the point of view of the evidence is that there isn't enough. Furthermore, the gospels are not consistent in their accounts of which events or specific teachings aroused or confirmed the determination of the leaders to be rid of him. If we are to be faithful to this evidence, it is not possible to tell the story as a whodunnit with a decisive emphasis on the conscious motivation of those who brought about his death.

Why then is the question pursued? One factor, I suspect, is a well-intentioned desire to counteract that strand of anti-semitism of which Christian history since the break with the synagogue seems never to have been entirely free. One form of reaction among Christians to this anti-semitic inheritance is the argument that it is unacceptable to hold the Jews as such responsible for Jesus' death. This argument is strengthened if it can be shown that the responsibility rested on the high-priestly caste of the day, whose credentials were extremely fragile, on Herod the contemptible upstart puppet, and on Pilate the imperial functionary. The embarrassing mention of the multitude who cried out, 'Crucify him!' can be distanced by talk of rent-a-crowd or, more patronisingly, by claiming that the multitude was misled. They did not know what they were doing.

This attempt to exonerate the Jews seems misguided in the sense that Jesus was a Jew, and the theological conflict which engaged him at its heart proceeded in a Jewish context. The claim that the Jews were not centrally caught up in his fate is therefore an odd one. But this has nothing to do with blame or recrimination, nor with any implication that we or any other group of people would have behaved differently in face of such a person.

A second strand involved in the investigation of why Jesus was killed is the desire to show that he met his death as a result of seeking direct confrontation with the powers that be. On this view his death was a consequence of his struggle against injustice and oppression. This Jesus is a non-violent revolutionary who paid for his convictions with his life at the hands of a religious and political establishment determined to preserve its own position at all costs. In view of the lack of evidence mentioned earlier, this interpretation reads like wishful thinking. Taken together the four gospels present a many-sided story, but there is no suggestion that Jesus sought to overthrow the regime of the day; nor yet that his enemies perceived him as seeking to do so.

It might still be objected that there is evidence, though fragmentary and not wholly consistent, in the evangelists' accounts of the 'trial' of Jesus. But the gospels are clear that Jesus was not arrested on suspicion. His arrest followed from a fully formed intention on the part of some at least of 'the leaders' to get rid of him. The trial is simply a means to that end. Precisely why this determination arose and was pursued to the end is not of central interest to the gospel writers. In this sense the 'whydunnit' approach, however intriguing, is a distraction from the task of interpreting the texts rather than a contribution to the elucidation of them.

In any case, to suppose that an answer is available to the question of why Jesus was put to death, is to take for granted a degree of rationality and coherence in these events which could hardly have been the case. I say this not out of a supposition that the situation around Jesus was especially prone to irrationality, but from observation of human crises. Once fear of destabilisation breaks out, the ways taken to avoid it or to prevent it spreading are not notably rational, whether in families, in small localised communities, or in the wider world. Nuclear deterrence exemplifies this spectacularly: the stock-piling of massive arsenals of weapons of a destructive potential entirely without precedent continues to be seriously and soberly defended as the best way of keeping the peace. More mundanely but no more rationally, the Lockerbie air crash and the Hillsborough football match disaster were each followed by a widespread compulsion to establish scapegoats as quickly and decisively as possible, even though in both cases information speedily and widely available suggested a very complex picture. What passed for rationality in these instances was the passionately-voiced conviction that such events must never happen again. We need not imagine that either those responsible for Jesus' arrest or those who sanctioned or went along with his crucifixion did so for any dispassionately worked-out purpose.

From the point of view of this book the most arresting aspect of the current quest to clarify why Jesus was killed is the assumption that there is here a conundrum to be solved. Jesus is taken to have been so obviously worthy and virtuous a person, a man whose watchwords in theory and practice were love and peace, that his crucifixion cries out for an explanation. In normal circumstances, it is implied, the killing of such a man would not have entered the heads of right-minded and well-intentioned persons.

It is this starting-point which must be called in question. What has such an image of Jesus to do with the man who said, 'I come to bring not peace but a sword', 'I have seen Satan fall like lightning from heaven', 'You brood of vipers!' and 'Get thee behind me, Satan!' – this last addressed to a very favoured disciple? The Jesus of the gospels is an extremely disturbing figure, frequently impatient, capable of intense anger, more than ready to give as good as he gets in polemical engagement with scribes and pharisees, unpredictable in terms of his availability to others and his responses to them; and finally committed to a seemingly self-destructive course which nobody around him could begin to understand.

He seems to come at the whole business of living and loving, hoping, fearing and dying from a place in himself which transcends universal and endemic anxieties but is as yet inaccessible to anyone else. A person who encourages a radically immature humanity to grow up by becoming like little children is not in the least comforting, reassuring or worthy of admiration to those wedded to their immaturity. Jesus provokes extreme reactions and at times encourages others to do their worst. His message to Herod is a model of imprudence: 'Go tell that fox . . . ' His response to Pilate is of no help in getting that wretched man off the hook, but is extremely provocative.

Though the evidence that he was not a zealot seems overwhelming, this conclusion is not to be equated with the idea that he was a pacifist or a believer in the way of non-violence in every circumstance. He both provoked violence and refused to exclude the violent from his sphere of concern. The zealots wanted to replace one regime with another, but Jesus called all regimes to account, not opposing any but seeing them all playing a significant part in the developing crisis and lacking any long-term security or guarantee. His refusal to be defined by any of these regimes, his claim to an origin, a call and a destiny beyond their control, was the most threatening thing about him.

Above all, clean contrary to the picture of a transparently good man who does what he has to do and simply becomes a victim of others' plotting, the gospels present Jesus as the one who has the initiative throughout, except when after the Last Supper he chooses to surrender it. The machinations of those who want to dispose of him are easily circumvented until the time comes when he makes them relevant by entering the city in such a way at so critical a moment instead of keeping a low profile. Even then they, like Pilate, are seen as instrumental to his purpose rather than the other way round. In this picture it is the one who surrenders who remains powerful, while the limit to the power of the supposedly powerful is embarrassingly exposed as they exhaust their power in the process of having him crucified.

In arguing on these lines that Jesus was not a good man I do not of course conclude that he was bad, but rather that the categories break down, or are broken open, in face of his story as we have it. Aquinas held that prudence was central to the moral life, and the author of Proverbs would almost certainly have agreed with him: 'A prudent man sees danger and hides himself; but the simple go on, and suffer for it'. Jesus did *both*, avoiding his enemies at Nazareth but asking for trouble by going up to Jerusalem at the time of the Passover Feast. He commends the combination: 'Be ye wise as serpents and as simple as doves.' Prudence has its place but if it becomes the lynch-pin of our morality it will involve great self-limitation, for it cannot guide the necessary surrender. That is where simplicity comes into its own, in the knowledge of when to be imprudent.

11

'Who Is My Mother?'

Under the heading 'Parents and Children' Karl Barth claimed without evidence that the gospel saying about hating your parents has to do with special and rare vocations. This is typical of the difficulty Christian thinkers have with such sayings, which tend to be mentioned rather gingerly as if they are at best in tension with more mainstream gospel teachings. The prevalent assumption within the Church is that the gospel is strongly in favour of the family. Yet the saying about hating our parents speaks of such hatred as a necessary condition for discipleship as such, and elsewhere in the gospel it is explicitly said that Jesus comes to divide people against one another, not least members of the same family.

The puzzle is intensified by consideration of gospel references to Jesus' attitude to his own family. Found in the Temple by his anxious parents he shows no recognition of their predicament: 'Why did you look for me? My place is here.' At Cana his first move is to resist his mother's suggestion that he should do something about the lack of wine at the marriage feast. Much later, when a woman in the crowd cries out in praise of his mother, he brushes her appreciation aside, using her words instead for his own immediate purpose: 'Blessed rather are those who hear the word of God and keep it!' Likewise, and most strikingly of all, when his mother and other family members are very concerned about him he reacts with brutal dismissiveness. 'Who is my mother? Who are my brethren? You are!', he says to those to whom he is speaking when the family message comes. Even if the incident at the crucifixion involving his mother and the beloved disciple is taken as an example of filial behaviour it stands in starkest contradiction to the decidedly unfilial attitude shown in the earlier incidents and vehemently commended in the sayings.

So far we have on the one hand an assumption that the gospel promotes harmonious family life at almost any price, and on the other a battery of texts which suggest the contrary. Far from being in favour of family life, it appears that Jesus rebelled against it and was prone not only to deny the family outright but to encourage others to do the same. Yet this polarity as it stands is tantalising rather than enlightening, and could easily lead to the conclusion that Jesus was commending nothing more interesting than doing your own thing in the manner of the existentialist philosopher. To leave it there is to allow a wrongly polarised form of the question to dictate the interpretation.

In his posthumously-published *Crucifixion–Resurrection*, E. C. Hoskyns provides a clue as to what more might be at stake. His argument is that the gospel affirms human relationships, not least the familial, but in a new way which frees them from an otherwise idolatrous self-sufficiency. This suggests to me that, just as a person is prone to be self-defining, so is a relationship or a network of relationships. In the necessary process of forging a familial identity every family is to some extent self-defined, deciding its own roles and purposes for each member. The temptation is to seek to sustain these regardless of wider vocational considerations or the exigencies and possibilities of situations beyond the family's ken. If not resisted at the point where it has become an obstacle to the individual member's growth beyond and outside the family, this self-defining thrust will paralyse and suffocate by denying those possibilities which are the air the emergent self needs to breathe. This denial of possibilities cripplingly restricts the future of individual members to what is within the particular family's present imaginative horizons.

To recognise this occupational hazard of being a family is salutary in a world where no society seems able to do without the family in some form or other; and where in our contemporary Western world family relationships are expected to bear a greater weight of conscious meaning and inter-personal significance than ever before. This heightening of expectation is often adduced in studies as a cause of divorce.

So far so good. But what has been said hardly accounts for the uniformly explosive tone of Jesus' reactions to the family. If what is at stake is no more than a cautionary tale, why does he consistently react this way? Why does his discipleship entail hatred of one's nearest relatives whether by marriage or by blood? This hyperbolic vehemence suggests a stern struggle *for him*. It is not so much the expectations his family may or may not have reposed in him but his own sense of identity and vocation that sets up this struggle. He is therefore at odds not with his family as such, but with whatever it is in him which would settle for their definition of him, which would be happy to allow their perfectly proper hopes and fears to dictate his course. The picture is not, however, that of a child seeking to throw off a grown-up tutelage now found oppressive. It is rather that of someone seeking to hold to his chosen course against the pull of everything in himself that would domesticate him, that would douse the fire in his belly by allowing him to retain a place in a self-sufficient world.

It is not therefore the family which is under attack but the conservative and even regressive potential of the family in one-self. What is at stake is what the individual makes of the family. The man who when called to follow Jesus says, 'I must first go and bury my father', exemplifies the predicament beautifully, and with maximum economy of words. It is possible to choose a familial identity which dictates the whole shape of my life. The maintenance of family relationships can become an absolute, and as such a destructive alternative to living your own life. The task of maintaining the family network in an immature and static form is ready to hand as an escape.

All human institutions develop a life of their own, a momentum which if it remains unredeemed will exert a killing power over those caught up in it. Are you scandalised when I say that the family is no exception to the rule? Indeed the rule applies with special force to those institutions, such as the family and the Roman Catholic Church, for which very distinctive theocratic claims are made. In any case, while the members are seen from within as having no existence beyond the family this may produce rebellion; it may equally spawn collusive members who for their own reasons want things to stay this way. To the extent that I am involved in such collusion I am in flight from my personhood.

Jesus' culture was one in which the family needed no defence, while simply to attack it in such a setting would have made no sense. I suggest that he takes the family for granted as a fact of life but resolutely refuses to define himself by it or to allow others so to define him. Similarly he goes out of his way to alert others to the necessary, painful and extremely dangerous ambiguity of the family which for all its creative and sustaining power has in it the capacity to be death-dealing. Perhaps the post-Freudian age has more ready access to this ambiguity and its implications for morality than earlier periods.

What matters most of all is that we are called into newness of life. But it is necessary to give some attention to the continuing effects of the condition *out of which* we are called. From within this condition, which Christian tradition has come to call original sin, it is impossible to see straight: we are in the grip of crooked seeing. Since nobody is completely free of this condition until everybody is, nobody sees completely straight.

Yet the condition which seems thus to trap us is historically formed and perpetuated: though universal and endemic it is not something that transhistorically pervades humanity, without beginning or end. It didn't just happen, and it doesn't have to continue to rule us. It was and is promoted by human beings. The temptation is to see it as simply part of what is given and unchangeable: part, if you like, of human nature itself. In fact it is precisely the dehumanising factor, that inexplicable pull against our becoming fully persons in a community of persons. It is from the starting-point of finding ourselves in this less-than-human state that we are called *into* the fullness of our humanity, not out of it.

The vital movement is a surrender to the unknown, or into the unknown, i.e. into a fullness of life simply unknown to and inconceivable by crooked seeing. The letting-go of my own life is a surrender into life. It must be so, because my own life as such has no meaning and indeed no reality. I am either one with all creation, linked indivisibly with everyone and everything else, or I am nothing but illusion. It is not that I exist only in relationship, it is that I *am* relationship from the beginning. At no point can I stand outside the web, for there is nowhere to stand. To think otherwise is to perpetuate the condition out of which we are called. In stressing this I should hope to avoid seeming to commend an easy existentialist rejection of family ties.

To rehearse in summary form the argument of this chapter, if the pattern of relationships within the family is looked at statically, growing up will be interpreted as rejection. The attempt to sustain in the individual a family-defined identity, ostensibly in the interests of love, restricts the flow of love by denying the revelation of personal identity. In such circumstances a lack of hatred would demonstrate a blunting of feeling, because there is never any neutrality and 'life will out'. Hatred, as the only authentic relational response available, keeps the venture alive and open to transcendence.

Any deficiency in love is a deficiency of identity. The passage out of this deficiency may well be through hatred, though not as a denial of love. Hatred is a sign of involvement, absolutely to be preferred to that numbing of feeling of which we need to be healed. Numbed feeling denies love, but hatred is a protest against the stunting of love.

There are families which are wholly self-defined and self-defining, and these have in effect sought to hold themselves in being outside the mystery. But every family has a built-in tendency towards this self-enclosure, and to the extent that it has gone this way a family becomes an object of hate.

Also worth considering in this connection is that strand of psycho-analytic thought which stresses the abiding effects of emotionally oppressive parental behaviour in people whose reactive feelings were repressed in childhood. The only way forward lies in gaining conscious access to those feelings the repression of which has left the person emotionally paralysed. If these emotions can be unburied and consciously claimed by means of a supportive/therapeutic relationship with a wise person who understands what is happening, the log-jam can begin to shift and more open horizons of relationship appear. The compulsive repetition of fixed patterns of emotional initiative and response established by the childhood trauma doesn't have to be the end of the story. But it must be stressed that there is no creative alternative to the recovery and reliving of the fear, anger, hatred and guilt repressed so long ago. It is incredible that any parent–child relationship could be entirely free of the distorting and restricting effects noted by Alice Miller and other post-Freudians. Here everyone has their story, and it is often those who appear most convinced of the happiness and normality of their childhood who have buried most.

To summarise the 'hard sayings' of Jesus as, 'Get in touch with your own feelings!' invites the charge of uncritical allegiance to fashionable psychological nostrums in the gospel's name. Yet if it is the case that recovery of particular repressed feelings supplies the key to the flourishing of my unique personhood, then encouragement to hate our parents becomes not only appropriate but crucial, at least as shorthand. What psycho-analytic thinking insists upon is that *the hatred is already there*: we have no choice about that after the repression. It is there in a subterranean form liable to distort quite unpredictably but in full accord with its own laws each and every relationship. So to encourage hating your parents is not to commend the introduction of some new element but rather to invite recognition of what is already there.

To say in the face of this that it is wrong to hate is not really a commendation of virtue but a refusal to acknowledge our present state and a reluctance to move beyond it. The conscious mind rules hatred out of court, or rather thinks to do so but lacks the power. Entrenched hatreds persist. There must be another way. Within a moralistic frame of reference the words of Jesus can only mean either, 'There is a duty to hate your parents,' or, 'Hating your parents is morally desirable and therefore to be aimed at'. The fact that these interpretations lack credibility shows that something is already wrong. This saying, like so many others, far from expressing either obligation or aspiration shows sharp attention to what is the case. In attending to the facts of our condition the saying invites us to see in them the inherent possibilities: an attainable freedom or continuing imprisonment.

From this standpoint the cauldron of exploitation, victimisation, oppression and trauma uncovered by psycho-analysis is precisely and in every particular the matter of our redemption. Once the trauma is released the story can be retold quite differently. It is not just a question of reliving hitherto repressed feelings, but of becoming attuned in that reliving to ever-present transcendence. Psycho-analytic theory and practice sometimes assume that memories remain the same throughout the process of recovery, and that they are wholly negative in content. By contrast, Christian faith proclaims the presence of the living God in every particular, yet in our thinking we habitually exclude from the effective sphere of divine presence and activity much that seems merely sordid and sad.

Full recovery of the emotions of childhood crisis can reverse this exclusion and separation. The ending of repression shows us the human predicament as both nightmarish and incandescent. Now trauma, which held us frozen in a closed world, dissolves into genuine tragedy, no longer needing drama or ritual, because open to the breath of life, the touch of God, the rebirth of all relationships in healing tears. Is not this the world which the Gospel reveals, the world in which and to which transfiguration is promised?

12

'If Anyone Does Not Hate . . .'

We try out different identities, and often get stuck with one or with a combination. So much of this is slavish imitation, or a series of pathetic attempts to be someone in the eyes of others. In any case it is not satisfying, because our real identity is beyond all that, given and yet to be discovered, waiting to be called out, to be exposed to trial and testing, to be honed into transparency.

The words of the song, 'Doesn't anybody know my name?' suggest a profound loneliness, which could be defined as having a name that goes unrecognised by others. But these haunting words could also mean that *I* don't know who I am: that my real identity is not clear to me, so that I need someone else to tell me who I am. Romantic imagining clings to the expectation that sooner or later the person will appear who in the perfection of complementarity will do just that. The more or less conscious insistence that the other person should understand me and show me to myself causes no end of trouble in intimate relationships. The failure of the other, I like to think, is that he or she doesn't adequately understand me and therefore doesn't tell me who I am with sufficient accuracy and comprehensiveness.

The persistence of this expectation of another human being is tragi-comic, for it fails to see that the chosen person has an exactly parallel dilemma in his or her own quest for identity. It seems that we do not and cannot give one another identity, though each can recognise and reverence in the other a mystery of unique personhood. As we are awakened, it begins to become possible to acknowledge the other as other rather than as a mere corroboration or revelation or extension of myself. But that is all.

The illusion that the other person can identify me is sometimes matched or even promoted by the chosen one's conviction that he or she has understood me. This is a recipe for oppression in relationship, for in the name of such imagined understanding the venture of reforming one's partner can proceed, often with the partner's collusion but at the expense of truth. Some of the seemingly harshest of Jesus' sayings stem, I suggest, from recognition of this blind alley. Insofar as familial and other relationships tend to involve me, long before I know what is happening, with versions of myself projected on to me by others a time comes when, if I am not to be trapped in a second-hand version of who I am or might be, I may even have to hate.

This hatred stems from a sense of my givenness as having a particular vocational thrust, a destiny not made to be encompassed by others' projections. This becomes properly and truthfully a matter of life and death, and hatred is preferable to indifference. Hatred at least recognises that at this critical juncture I do not cease to be in relationship, whereas indifference implicitly denies all that. It could be that if we don't care enough to hate at times we shall never learn to love. What is being said is not that hatred is a good thing in a sense equivalent to the gospel commendation of love, but that we may have to pass through hatred on our way in to mature love.

It has to be emphasised that the freedom at issue is a freedom in relationship, not an escape from relationship into the cultivation of emotional and spiritual indifference to others. This means that at times the only available emotion will be hatred, and that it is at those times vital to let this be the case rather than to fly from it. Hatred is a sign of involvement, but frustrated involvement. It is love unable to find consummation. Jesus is not, then, commending some life-denying form of holiness but the single-minded pursuit of the task of becoming my true self.

Jesus is not a professional ascetic with a down on intimate relationships. He is rather a promoter or catalyst of the kind of breaks which have to be made if we are to grow into our full stature. If I can't make these breaks, my name is still sadly far to seek. To allow no place for hatred can end only in unnamed unreality.

13

'Where Your Treasure Is . . .'

The sayings considered in this book invite into a life which cannot be imagined, still less understood, ahead of or aside from that surrender which is the way in to it. Yet this is a life which is already in us. In us but unknown to us and therefore threatening, frightening, with its intimation of no way back to ego-security. From the point of view of the outcome who would want to go back? Who would prefer being Solomon in all his glory (ego-achievement) to being one of the lilies of the field (spontaneous flourishing)? But the process of change is unnerving.

The point about surrender is made most poignantly in the context not of relationships but of possessions, in the story of Jesus and the rich young man. It has been said that the conflict between rich and poor is essentially a matter of human anxiety. Possessions are necessary 'because there are those who feel they are nothing without them'. Jesus' words, 'Woe to you that are rich, for you have received your consolation', thus cease to be seen as condemnatory and are understood instead as a cry of compassion for the plight of the rich. Those who have nothing but their possessions already face an emptiness which cannot be filled. The Greek text has the sense of 'Alas for you' rather than 'Woe to you'. The gospel story of the rich young man has always seemed to me to strike a note not of condemnation but of overwhelming sadness, a sadness indivisibly of the man himself and of Jesus.

It is sometimes *in our very virtue* that our doom lies. It is not that virtue is an illusion, but that it is not saving. If I am to preserve my moral integrity by always doing what the rigorous voice of duty commands, what place is there for faith, hope and love? I do not need these gifts, for I have my integrity – a barren thing. By contrast, 'Let the dead bury their dead,' are words so offensive to the Jewish religious outlook of Jesus' time that E. P. Sanders concludes that Jesus must have uttered them, there being no other conceivable reason why this saying should appear in the gospel text! My purpose in quoting the saying here is to stress that while virtue has its place it is not an alternative to the gift and call of God. The way of virtue did not satisfy the rich young man, and his dissatisfaction looked for another step. Jesus responded, 'Sell all you have, give to the poor and come, follow me.'

Can you imagine the shock of this invitation? The man is asked to abandon not just wealth but security, power and geographical stability in order to follow a wanderer without assets or credentials. Is such a course compatible either with moral prudence or with sanity? How can it be defended in terms of service of others? This man is implicitly asked to give up the power of doing good. This power to continue to be a benefactor is something very many find hard to surrender, and others to admit they do not have.

In any case the young man was being asked to leave behind a whole taken-for-granted world in the interests of nothing and nobody except Jesus. Yet it was *the man's own dissatisfaction* with the way of virtue which he had followed up to then that prompted this response from Jesus. The man's tragedy was that he could not take the break-out that was on offer. Jesus offered all he could: the way *he* was on. It was no more reasonable or responsible of him to have made the offer than it would have been for the young man to have accepted it. But the implication of the story is not that what deterred the man was the irresponsibility or madness of Jesus' invitation. It was rather that he could not bring himself to let go of his 'great possessions'. As long as he was tied to his possessions and what they represented he could neither soar nor plunge into the strange new space put before him. 'Where your treasure is, there will your heart be also'; there was nothing more that Jesus could do.

It is like having the chance of learning to ride a bicycle but needing first to take off the roller-skates which have served you so well for so long. The thought of being without roller-skates might in such an instance be devastating: no mobility, and an as yet unrideable bicycle totally beyond your control. The young man was unable to face that lostness, that vulnerability, that condition of being a child again. This incident, then, is about the dissatisfaction of a thoroughly virtuous person who nevertheless cannot find release from an identity which binds him, in his case that of having great possessions.

His possessions shield him from exposure and so prove life-denying. He remains hung up on what he has to the extent of not being able to come into touch with who he is. He can't let go of the fearful identity of the possessor who, by insisting on his ownership in face of the life-affirming invitation of Jesus, builds against death and so misses the freedom of the universe.

What is exemplified is how easily and even imperceptibly possessing becomes being possessed. The young man's problem is not his possessions but the fact that they possess him. The story should therefore not be used, though it frequently is, as a kind of gospel charter for a Christian policy towards the poor. If nothing else sufficiently shaking happened subsequently in this man's life, he would have found himself facing death still possessed by his possessions. His coldest of comforts would be that he had kept all he owned. The onset of death would have rendered his carefully husbanded possessions meaningless. There is the realisation, at once terrifying and liberating, that there is nothing there. This can be expressed in perhaps overly schematic form by saying that all human hope must come to nothing, and must be recognised to have come to nothing, if theological hope is to come into its own.

14

'Come, Follow Me'

The calling of the first disciples, at least in Mark's version, was sudden and abrupt. Jesus called them to follow him, and they did so on the instant. A theological student understandably found this a bit much: 'He must have already known them, and they him. Otherwise he was behaving very irresponsibly.' This example makes very explicit our tendency to confine the story of Jesus within our categories of acceptable behaviour. The attempt is threadbare because all the evidence not only of this text but of the whole thrust of the gospel story suggests that Jesus was irresponsible. Here we have someone who uproots and re-routes people, taking them right out of their existing securities and leading them nowhere. If that isn't irresponsible, what is?

Counsel for the defence might argue that these people whom Jesus took on a three-year trip and then left in a shadow-land were of adult age and free to choose. He was not in a position to coerce them. Why visit exclusively on him their fecklessness and folly? He seems to have had his own rather eccentric priorities, but they were the people who had responsibilities which were instantly abandoned at his call. The worst that Jesus could reasonably be charged with would be encouraging their irresponsible behaviour, of which he could be said to have been the occasion but certainly not the source or cause. We don't blame the raggle-taggle gypsies for the fact that the lady of the castle went off with them.

But the story as we have it presents Jesus as the one who had the initiative, so the view that it is always the strongest who is to blame would apply. In any case to charge him with collusion in others' irresponsibility is enough to make the point that Jesus was irresponsible. A wiser or more mature person would surely have discouraged so hasty a response. To promote the disruption of the lives not only of these individuals but of their families in exchange for a totally uncertain future finds no justification in any of the dearly bought conventions of civilised human intercourse.

There are devices for taking the edge off this sense of the wildness of Jesus' behaviour. One is to say that he was ushering in the Kingdom, or at least drawing urgent attention to the fact that it was being inaugurated. But the concept of the Kingdom normally invoked to legitimise this bizarre behaviour remains opaque and lifeless. An extension of this unsatisfactoriness into discussion of particular moral questions is the use of the phrase 'kingdom values'. Such an expression is hardly in the same universe of discourse as Jesus' declared intent of casting fire upon the earth.

A cruder tactic is to remind everyone that Jesus was God. This is done for the dubious purpose of claiming that behaviour which would not normally be acceptable is so in this singular instance. The implication is that by definition whatever Jesus said and did was not only legitimate but laudable. The behaviour looks odd, but of course he was God. To argue thus is to abandon the search for intelligibility in the behaviour. It is to give up any serious interest either in what was going on between Jesus and his chosen ones or in the implications of calling on his name today. To play the divinity card in this way is to cheat rather than to challenge.

If on the other hand we picture Jesus as someone uniquely and overwhelmingly awake to the love that is poured out and passionately centred on the urging of that divine love his behaviour looks quite different. He will be seen as sparing nothing to prompt others into a comparable awakening, for on such an awakening depends the creative outcome of the human adventure. There is in humanity the stubborn hope of an unimaginable human flourishing, a hope that refuses to die despite the vast scale of physical, psychological and spiritual destruction amongst us that seems to belie it. Jesus dares to call that hope out of hiding.

Behaviour which from one point of view can only be described as irresponsible can from another angle be seen as decisive in claiming our destiny as human persons born to be children of the living God. 'Like lightning flashing from the east even unto the west, so shall the coming of the Son of Man be.' On the supposition that the impact of Jesus on those who in due course became his first disciples was of this order, his abrupt call and their startlingly immediate response make sense. Or rather, that is so on an assumption that his power is liberating rather than manipulative. Some Christian apologists would argue that this assumption is shown by the eventual outcome to be correct; but this argument invites the countercharge of complacency. The Christian record is a very mixed bag, and unspeakable things not only have been done but continue to be done in Jesus' name.

It is best to concede this last argument and to be grateful for it, at least as a salutary reminder that not all issues are resolved by the raising of Jesus from the dead. As long as the story is unfinished, and perhaps only in its beginnings, it is unwise of us who in our lives are part of its further telling to claim univocal achievements either for present-day Christianity or for our for-bears in faith. To appeal to any eventual outcome imagined as already having happened is gravely to distort the story by dismembering it. This dismembering has as one of its effects a rather wishful denial of so much present ambiguity. Another and possibly even more serious effect is to diminish our sense of open horizons in the present, and the opportunity and responsi-bility therein contained.

To return to the calling of the first disciples and how oddly it sits with everyday notions of responsibility. Until we have experienced a comparable disturbance of our habitual ways it is unlikely in any case that we shall have much to the purpose to say about the behaviour of Jesus or the disciples at that moment. If we have not been electrified, or are resisting being electrified, we are bound to take a somewhat negative or at best a distant view of this and other gospel incidents. Indeed if such stories were to be told of anyone other than Jesus we should hardly hesitate to speak of irresponsibility, probably of folly and perhaps even of derangement.

How is it then that such stories continue to be read and re-read in church without any discernible shock-effect? Presumably it is a mental trick whereby we make of Jesus a special case, in such a way that no question of invitation or identification can arise with any degree of seriousness. If those theologians are right who see sin as a condition of distorted seeing in which we are all involved, and if those psychologists are right who claim that our society spawns and perpetuates myths of such appalling inhumanity that those who can't or won't conform to them are not infrequently driven into madness, then it would be expected that those who are in touch with or awakened to the mystery would be readily judged irresponsible at best.

For Christians to decry such judgements on Jesus and his first followers without examining their own presuppositions about present discipleship is mindless. The gospel cries out for the reassessment of all our thinking on what is responsible and what is not. In the image of the lilies of the field those nagging anxieties about past, present and future that so largely rule our lives are of no account. To be without such burdens is unimaginable, yet it is what Jesus commends. It is not a question of the reduction of the human being to a plant-like state, for this freedom in humanity has to do with faith. Kierkegaard's reminder that the opposite of sin is not virtue but faith is apposite here. Freedom from sin is not achieved by striving to build up the defences of virtuous habit against its inroads, but by a believing which means the desiring of such freedom. The only way is to believe that sin's power is at an end because 'our sins are nailed to the Cross with Christ.' This believing means desiring such freedom with every fibre of my being.

As we cease to carry our own burden we can afford to be irresponsible in the sense that Jesus and the first disciples were. 'Why don't we walk ourselves instead of carrying ourselves?' a friend asked recently. It is a question of the *kind of life* that is available to us and for which we are destined. Our fetters have to be beginning to break and our burden to lift before we can see this newness of life, this overflowing as either possible or desirable. The gospel presents it as both. Awakened faith sees it as both. Sin can see no reality in it, for sin always looks to the withholding of the self.

Jesus could work no wonders in Nazareth, the place of his youth, because the people there had no faith in him. There was an understandable reluctance to believe that he had anything to offer. By contrast, at the wedding in Cana, those whom he told to fill up the wine-jars with water found themselves doing what he said. In thus responding they became part of the sign. It's never just Jesus on his own. It's always the meeting of faith with faith. He looks to a responsive faith, and when he finds it things take off, as in the call of the disciples.

From the outside it looks irresponsible. The question is not how I might or might not have responded had I been there but how I now respond. Where does the telling of the first disciples' story leave me? Does my present self-understanding give me a place in that story or not? If not, is that because my call has not ripened, or because such calls are fantasy, or because I am in flight from the voice I need to hear? Nobody else can answer that question for me.

15

'You Will All Be Scandalised . . .'

Jesus' description of the dire fate of the bringer of scandal to the little ones caught my imagination in childhood and has never left me. The consequences for such a person would be even worse than finding himself at the bottom of the sea with a millstone tied round his neck. This could only mean eternal damnation, I assumed; while what scandal itself was remained unclear. Later I was taught that scandal means something that trips up or ensnares. Moralistic examples abounded of the ways in which we influence one another, culminating in the cautionary tale put before us with pious horror that while one bad orange in a box can turn all the others bad the reverse is not the case. Since one implication of all this was that to be scandalised was not merely to be shocked but to have the course of your life drastically altered, it seemed to leave goodness a very fragile plant.

Such doom-laden strictures appeared alien to the gospel spirit, so the theme remained quite unresolved in the margins of my mind until my attention was drawn to another range of texts. The most mind-blowing of these is Jesus' interpretation of the psalmist's words: 'The very stone which the builders rejected has become the cornerstone.'

Jesus' commentary is brief and stark: 'Everyone who falls on that stone will be broken to pieces; but when it falls on anyone it will crush him' (Luke 20:17–18). This cornerstone is one to whom everybody must relate. There is no avoiding this encounter. Here, then, is a startlingly new angle on the topic of scandal. The image is reversed. No longer is the bringer of scandal judged and found wanting; contrariwise, it is the rock of stumbling that is the criterion.

The notion of the imitation of Christ has played a recurrent part in Christian history. The problem of imitation is more rarely noticed but becomes sharply evident if we are imitating one who brings scandal to others. In this context imitation cannot be anything obvious. Pursuit of this less-than-obvious sense of imitation is central to this book.

The tension between two seemingly contradictory and mutually exclusive images of scandal is not eased if our present text is seen as an echo, as it surely must be, of the Lord's words to the prophet in Isaiah (8:12–14):

> 'Do not call conspiracy all that this people call conspiracy, and do not fear what they fear, nor be in dread. But the Lord of hosts, him you shall regard as holy; let him be your fear, and let him be your dread. And he will become a sanctuary, and a stone of offence, and a rock of stumbling to both houses of Israel, a trap and a snare to the inhabitants of Jerusalem.'

Here it is quite explicit that it is the Lord who is both the one over whom people trip and the one who ensnares them. It is intriguing to note in addition that the one who is thus pictured is also said to be a sanctuary. Contradiction upon contradiction.

It is in its application to Jesus himself that the theme of the scandaliser comes into its own, finding a meaning and a resonance way beyond mere horror images and cautionary tales. The key is to apply both kinds of text together, those which stress the fate of the bringer of scandal and those which make him the criterion. Then and only then can we be hit by the full force of what Jesus does with this image. Whatever offence he gives to the religious and moral sensibilities of the day he is scandalous in the much deeper and more decisive sense that he goes on a way which his own, those who have left all and followed him, can in no sense follow. Matthew (26:31) records Jesus as saying, 'You will all be scandalised this night because of me': the bridge-passage, the place where the meaning of the scandal-bringer is redefined, is the Passion.

It is worth noting in passing that our customary translations of this verse do not bring out the resonance. I owe it to the Rheims–Douay version of my childhood, here more faithful to the original than either the Revised Standard Version's 'fall away because of me' or the Jerusalem Bible's 'lose faith in me', the former a watering down and the latter a distortion. These translations are themselves indicative of the difficulty in coming to terms with Jesus as scandalous to believers.

It is the 'little flock', those of his special choosing, who are most immediately and directly scandalised to see him opting for and suffering the fate of the bringer of scandal. To be drowned

with a millstone is a fate much less inhumane than to be crucified. Thus my childhood speculation about what would happen
to the giver of scandal is answered by the crucifixion of Jesus.
'Do not call conspiracy all that this people call conspiracy, and
do not fear what they fear . . . ' It is about perception, and more
specifically that shift from crooked to straight seeing so central
in conversion. It is, in the first instance, those who have projected
all their hopes and dreams on to Jesus and his mission who are
necessarily and decisively ensnared by his plunge into darkness.

'It is necessary that stumbling-blocks come, but woe to the
man by whom they come.' My argument is that to be scandalised
by Jesus is inescapable if he is to have any decisive purchase on
our hearts and minds. To be thus tripped up is to encounter
him as the uprooting of us, as the reduction of us to nothing,
and not being able to take it. There is no straight transition from
unregenerate notions of security, power and well-being into the
way of Jesus. The trap is in the strong disjunction between the
prior direction of our life and the stone's impact. This dislocation
is appropriately imaged as being broken to pieces, being crushed
or being ensnared. It is the breaking open of the hard outer shell
upon which we depend so deeply that we may be scarcely or
not at all aware of the vast energies engaged in sustaining it.
From the point of view of that which is twisted the impact of
that which is straight can only be scandalous. There has to be
scandal if there is to be new life.

'Let him [the Lord] be your fear, and let him be your dread.'
The whole of our life can helpfully be seen as a movement from
terror to love. There is terror in the face of life from long before
we can remember. This terror easily and unawares becomes
endemic, making us desperate survivors putting a brave face on
things rather than vessels of praise and glory. Terror is at the
root of our deep resistance to change and our inability to believe
that we can be changed. It has been said that the transition out
of this terror into love is always accompanied by fear of the
Lord.

This fear is an awakening to the mystery. It lets God be God
beyond human wisdom or control. It insists on the unnerving
sense that Jesus is always ahead of us, though not as dominating
or superior. He is rather a continuing scandalous invitation to
fathom more fully the dissolving ways of our healing and thus
to come integrally into touch with our feelings and imaginings.
Precisely here is matter for transfiguration, but such stuff must

first be reclaimed from buried depths, honoured and offered. The scandal which this chapter examines thus spells the unlearning of terror and the initiation into the fear of the Lord which accompanies our rebirth in love.

In *The Denial of Death* Ernest Becker draws attention to 'the destructive toll that our pretense of sanity takes'. Thomas Merton writes similarly of the colonisers of the Renaissance, whom he sees as alienated from themselves and therefore imposing on primitive worlds 'their own confusion and their own alienation'. My claim is that the stone of stumbling puts this whole tragic story into reverse in the individual and through the individual in the race.

In shattering my hard shell he makes buried energies available for reconciliation with my victims, not least with myself. This scandal-bringer gives the lie to life-long strategies of undying survival and of imagined control over life. The urgent, compulsive striving to get my act together and to keep my show on the road is exposed in all its pathetic vanity and heartless, uncentred hopelessness by the impact of the stone. Once I am truly tripped or crushed nothing can ever be the same again, for the escape-mechanisms to which I am habituated, the forms of my flight from reality, are revealed for what they are. This revelation is a severe but benevolent form of being found out, being seen to be not at home, at odds with and very far away from my true self. It is not condemnatory, for as I am shown with unerring accuracy my present predicament, now clear for the first time, there is already the fresh possibility and promise of another way. I am no longer doomed to the repetitive pattern of my unfreedom in which, strong in the eyes of others, I am prisoner to the compulsion to make of another person or a job or a situation my whole identity. Becker writes of 'the other as one's whole world, just as the home really is for the child'. The scandaliser will have none of this and so goes to great lengths to show me what in this driven state I have made of myself.

This theme has very wide bearings. Yeats was on to something when he saw the sleeping centuries 'vexed to nightmare by a rocking cradle'. Far from all issues being already resolved by the resurrection, it is from then on that the death of the beloved begins to work its way in this world. The presence and the sign of this death in the world is destabilising. It is so by bringing us to the place in ourselves where we are undefended, the place of homecoming, the place of God, the place in which we may not have dwelt fully since infancy, the place from which we are habitually absent and yet most deeply desire to inhabit.

The story does not end here, for the priority placed on our being tripped up by Jesus is not for its own sake. It is that we in our turn may become the stone of stumbling. Everything that he was and is we are to become. The claim that where two or three are gathered together the risen Lord is in the midst of them is subversive, for it implies that the principalities and powers are thereby put on the defensive.

With this in mind let us briefly rehearse some aspects of the story, beginning with the brilliant epitome of the whole thing furnished by the juxtaposition of two sentences in the Christmas liturgy:

> The Lord said to me: 'You are my son, this day I have begotten you.' Why do the nations fret, and the people cherish vain dreams?

The alignment suggests that the fretting and overheated imagining referred to are provoked by the emergence in our midst of this particular person. The presence of this person, quite apart from any conscious intent or lack of intent on his part, was disturbing. From the beginning, despite or perhaps because of angels, shepherds and wise men, there is this fretting, first manifested in Herod's initial uneasiness about the rumoured child. The liturgical placing of the slaughter of the innocents within the Christmas season is a master-stroke which we make nothing of while continuing to complain that our society makes of Christmas something merely sentimental and commercial. If it is true that the situation produced Jesus in that there is a certain fittingness about the time and place of his coming, it is equally true that his presence presses the situation towards overt crisis. It is too easy to hold the other actors in the drama responsible for all the seemingly negative things that happened.

Once what we solemnly call the public life of Jesus gets under way, the fretting continues with rising intensity. In the climacteric the ranks close against this bewildering bearer of new life who has appeared from nowhere and now threatens by his presence to render an extremely fraught religious and political situation uncontrollable from the leaders' point of view. The religious leaders come to see that the thrust of Jesus' mission threatens the continuance of their role, and especially the fragile stability of their accommodation with the occupying power. But the form of threat he presents differentiates him from other messianic claimants. Jesus is not campaigning to replace either the Roman imperial jurisdiction or religious domination by the worldly-wise with the reign of the true Israelites, the pure and the pious. He is not and does not need to be merely against the government, for his concern is not focused there. What makes him a danger is the contagiousness of his perception that even now the power that matters is not in the hands of ruling elites. The people meanwhile are restless and their reactions brittle: they acclaim Jesus on his donkey-ride but within days lend support to his condemnation.

As to his own immediate chosen followers, they are nowhere very much. It means little to call them unfaithful, for what in practice would have counted as fidelity on their part? But the form of their disarray shows that they were not at one with Jesus. Having looked to him and followed him thus far they too are now part of the fretting, their vain dreams of precedence in the kingdom having earlier evoked Jesus' rebuke. As in all these stories there is no evidence to suggest that at the time they understood their mistake. The specific form of their being scandalised by Jesus has to do with the fact that they had already put their faith in him, as he acknowledged at the supper. His way of life through death, which by identification with him was to become the keynote of Christian faith, was beyond them until they had been through their own form of disillusionment. Then and only then could they be one with him. It is childish and complacent to say that they should have known better when they did not understand his journey into death.

16

'He That Shall Lose His Life . . .'

Feminism, anti-racism and all other currents of thought opposed to the oppression of particular kinds of people seem to want to rule out victimhood. Christian faith by contrast has an image of chosen victimhood at its very heart. Does this mean that those many Christians vigorously involved in anti-oppression movements are in error?

This question can be approached by consideration of the gospel saying, 'He that shall lose his life shall find it'. If we are not merely to rest in paradox we have to ask what this life is that must be lost in order to be found. Alternatively, is the life that is to be lost the same as the life that is to be found? Liberation movements see a contrast between a slavish or other-directed life and a free or self-determined life: their concern is to promote movement from the former to the latter. It could perhaps be said that the slavish life is the life we have to lose if the life of freedom is to be found. Each could be said to be my life since I am in some sense the same person throughout, who finds in each of these lives successively a certain identity.

The reflections of a forty-year-old woman emerging from long and deep depression might seem to confirm this interpretation without her knowing it:

> The world has not changed. There is so much evil and mean-ness all around me, and I see it even more clearly than before. Nevertheless, for the first time I find life really worth living. Perhaps this is because, for the first time, I have the feeling that I am really living my own life. On the other hand, I can understand my suicidal ideas better now -- it seemed pointless to carry on – because in a way I had always been living a life that wasn't mine, that I didn't want, and that I was ready to throw away.

The movement here is from a just-one-thing-after-another life, a second-hand life shaped in the formative years by the limits set by others' real or imagined expectations, into living her own life. How neatly this appears to fit with Jesus' words about life needing to be lost in order to be found! This woman has sloughed off her second-hand life and found her own life. The example is so vivid and telling that no more, it would seem, needs to be said.

The picture can be filled out by other examples. A nun said to me with great insistence: 'Very few of us ever leave home!' She meant human beings. If we take leaving home as an image of the movement already described, her view might at once confirm the wisdom of Jesus' words and suggest the comparative rarity in practice of the development he commends. This cautionary note has its place, for it is easy to be naive about how this change is accomplished, as indicated by the remark of another friend, also a member of a religious community: 'We used to think we could leave our parents simply by getting on a train and joining the monastery!' Others, I suspect, think they can leave home just by getting married, or ordained, or moving to another place. It turns out to be not so simple, as the following personal example may indicate.

Having lived in many places far from home, I decided recently to go away and spend ten days entirely alone. I had often been alone before but had always been afraid of being alone for long. This time I *chose* that isolation which I had hitherto most dreaded. It somehow seemed necessary. During those days it was shown to me with a peaceful clarity beyond contradiction that my whole life had been ruled by fear.

This was a fear not of anything in particular but of somehow getting things wrong: a sense of having always to be constrained and guarded, apparently because of the limits set by other people's expectations – initially, and overwhelmingly, parental expectations; then school, then society. I am speaking of a fearful conformity, a sort of interiorised reign of terror which had nothing to do with any obvious cruelty done to me or threatened to me by anyone. In retrospect it had everything to do with my collusion with a voice which said subliminally, 'Whatever you do you must not lead your own life'; or, more accurately and cuttingly, 'You have no life of your own to lead. You are nothing.' This meant that I had thus far led a life of subjection. To see it so clearly was already to be moving out of it or to be being moved out of it. That life of subjection was, it now seemed, the life I had to lose if I was ever to live. This recognition drew me further and further into the process of losing a life to gain one.

What then of Jesus, if we see his teaching as a commentary on his own story? He is remembered as the one who came that we human beings might have life, and have it more abundantly. The story of his baptism, especially the voice saying, 'You are my beloved Son. With you I am well pleased,' reads like a conversion experience. The time had come when he was to cease living the subject life he had lived for thirty years and begin to live his own life. That is the thrust of the story, rather dehumanised by the use of staid phrases like, 'He now began his public ministry.' Henceforward he claims and enters upon his destiny. His life of subjection, indispensable as formative, has served its turn.

The life of subjection, if inappropriately prolonged, becomes a life without personal shape or purpose. In middle life I needed to be set free from an inability or refusal to leave home. But it must be emphasised that to live my own life is not at all the same as to be rebellious, to be wilfully 'doing my own thing'. The trouble with rebellion is that it is merely the other side of the coin of conformity. It is a desperate attempt to establish your difference, still totally ruled by others' expectations in the form of your need to defy them. Put in group terms, rebellion is part of the condition of being in the dependent group. In this archaic dynamic individuality has no place. Rebellion, like conformity, lacks the originality of living your own life. It is this originality which Jesus exemplifies. Jesus' originality made him at the time both compellingly attractive and impossible.

So far so good. On the face of it we have a tidy correspondence between our own vocational development, the story of Jesus, and the saying of Jesus about losing and finding your life. As to victimhood, on this analysis it would seem to be a dimension of being under the sway of what I have called the second-hand life. Part of what is given up in the movement into living my own life is precisely the sense of myself as doomed to be always at others' beck and call, a condition which until then I may well not have recognised as that of being a victim.

Yet here at last doubts must arise as to the finality and even the adequacy of the parallels I have so far drawn. Stubbornly present at the very centre of what the New Testament tells us about Jesus is his choice of victimhood 'even unto death'. Far from contradicting what has been said about his emergence from the years of subjection, it is precisely in the time of emergence that this victim-destiny is affirmed and held to by Jesus against the vehement rejection of any such prospect for him, expressly by Peter and implicitly by others of the chosen. This recalcitrant factor at the heart of the story breaks open the pattern I have so far presented, introducing a quite other dimension not matched in my alleged parallels.

It seems that the life that is to be lost is precisely the life Jesus has found in his conversion. This is a life that of its nature cannot be clung to in ego-control but can only be surrendered, or at least voluntarily put at risk. It is as if this life cannot declare its true meaning except in and through this surrender. The freedom to live his own life turns out to involve embracing death. Not that this implies a suicidal or accident-prone habit of mind: in his own time and way he enacts the death which is in store for him, the point being graphically made in his earlier message to Herod when the latter was thought to be seeking to kill him: 'Go and tell that fox, "Behold, I cast out demons and perform cures today and tomorrow, and the third day I finish my course." ' Jesus is presented as choosing the place of ultimate weakness, so that although he undoubtedly meets his end at the hands of others and comes at it through profound turmoil of spirit he is not an unwilling victim in the ordinary sense.

The movement here is of converted or first-hand life into surrender, indeed into the ultimate surrender. This is the 'catch' from the point of view of those who see the Gospel as merely against oppression. The oppressed state which is a partial outcome of the dependent condition is itself a part of the dynamic of our salvation, at least if looked at from the viewpoint of developmental conflict. It has always seemed to me breathtaking that Jesus not only accepted that Judas was to betray him but encouraged him to do so. A clue as to why, when the time comes, he encourages not only Judas but through him all the forces which bear enmity to him is provided by Sebastian Moore. If Jesus represents humanity made whole, evil desirous of his death is evil on the verge of redemption. Our evil understood as our thrust against wholeness exposes us to the love of God 'in a way and at a depth to which even our desire for wholeness does not expose us'. Evil desires its own transformation but enters into the total transformation only through crucifying Jesus.

There is something unfathomable here which must not be

ignored or distanced if serious distortion of the gospel is to be avoided. Remember also that Exodus says that the Lord hardened Pharaoh's heart against the Israelites, and Acts puts into the mouth of Peter after the resurrection the strong conviction that Jesus' enemies acted in accordance with some divine design when they killed him. Notions of primary and secondary causality, or of the permissive will of God, are often invoked in an attempt to come to terms with such claims, but they are no better than a distraction into a mental world quite alien to our witnesses and to the whole spirit of the story of salvation. So much for the mysterious nexus between God and evil.

Only the life of someone really living his or her own life can become a story of true self-love and therefore of self-gift. This is a life apt to be lost, whose nature is to be yielded up. Without prejudice to what has been said about our need to get beyond a life of subjection, such a life is not after all the focus of the particular words of Jesus which this chapter seeks to expound. At issue in these words is that further dimension of the story wherein I am shown my life as a gift to be given. The paradox is that it is only the life which is genuinely found which can be, and which desires to be, given away.

Confirmatory of the reality of this dimension is the story of Etty Hillesum, told in her diary and letters and corroborated by others who knew her. She was a Dutch Jewess in her mid-twenties as the Nazi occupiers' drive against Jewish people in Holland moved into top gear. She was surrounded by Jews in the grip of fear, resentment, fatalism, or the illusion – clearly seen as such by Etty – that the Western allies would somehow prevent the cataclysm which loomed. She wrote:

> I only want to be true to that in me which seeks to fulfil its promise . . . I have matured enough to assume my 'destiny', to cease living an accidental life . . . It is no longer a romantic dream or the thirst for adventure, or for love, all of which can drive you to commit mad and irresponsible acts. No, it is a terrible, sacred, inner seriousness, difficult and at the same time inevitable.

Later Etty left for Auschwitz singing.

Deeply present but still implicit in this story, and explicit in the story of Jesus, is a strong notion of obedience, not in the corrupted and diminished modern sense of just doing what you are told, but as a key function of relationship indivisibly with

the living God and with all that is. True obedience has conno-
tations of listening, of receptivity, of honouring the other in his
or her sheer otherness. It is only the person who is living his or
her own life who is capable of obedience in this sense. This
essentially non-coercive obedience has to be learned, and can
only be learned in the testing exercise of the freedom of authentic
personhood.

It is revealing to note that Jesus is said to have learned obedience by suffering, that is to say by passionately taking the consequences of his own decision to pursue his destiny in the way
that he did. If we think of suffering simply as something imposed
upon him by his enemies we miss the point to which this chapter
necessarily keeps returning: there is in play here a chosen and
offered suffering, a suffering therefore in a category quite other
than that which is sheerly imposed and endured. It is not at all
a case of 'what can't be cured must be endured,' but of a willing
plunge into this particular suffering which once accomplished
turns out to be healing. Having once happened it has become
rooted not only in the mind and imagination of the race but in
the very heart of the earth, so that for all that has yet to be
resolved nothing can ever be the same again.

The way of faith, hope and love is hinted at in Jesus' references
to the Father's will and Etty's to her 'destiny'. The convergence
between the two is striking: both manifest an awesome faithful-
ness in pursuit of a call which is also a gift, and which points
towards death. Neither is understood by those around them, but
each is totally involved in the people, though no utilitarian
calculus could conceivably suggest a fruitful outcome for the
chosen course.

Something said earlier must now be called in question. Contrary to what this chapter may have seemed to claim, what is
at stake is not a continuity of personhood from oppression to
liberation but a coming into being of myself. This coming into
being involves more than, and mysteriously other than, liberation from the oppressors. It is axiomatic throughout this book
that human nature is always in a state of becoming, not of being.
The point now to be made is that human becoming involves a
necessarily painful and problematic emergence from a condition
of *desired dependence* which is also characteristically oppressive.
Notice also that the movement is not from dependence to auton-
omy, but from immature to mature forms of dependence.

Of course oppression as such is not desirable: it is to be

opposed. But the oppressed condition remains a factor in our present experience, playing its providential role as part of what is, and thus inviting chosen victimhood. The fact that we never simply get away from dependence has as one of its consequences that we never entirely avoid oppression. It follows that to move in thought from becoming to being, from emerging liberation to a state of fully achieved freedom, is to move from faith to fantasy, and destructive fantasy at that. A spectacular example of this movement is provided by Maximilien de Robespierre, a man of undoubted and profound ideals, who was brought by the fantasy of achieved freedom to preside over the Terror. Complacent strictures on the French Revolution serve rather to conceal than to illuminate this tragic shift of consciousness.

A reflection on Christian ministry may illustrate the point. One fashionable image of such ministry current in theological training is of a life of selfless enabling. Implicit in this image is the assumption that the minister's selfhood is of no account: what matters is that he or she should help others to be or to become themselves. Here ministry is being defined by an ideal-ised and therefore unrelated self, so that the picture which emerges is of a ministry which, for all its claim to an overriding concern for others, is non-relational and therefore manipulative.

I want by contrast to suggest that all you have to give is yourself. Yes, yourself redeemed, graced, in process of transform-ation; but still yourself, the you that no one else can be. You are not made to become an enabling machine but a loving, unique person; and these are decisively different images of what ministry is, and ultimately of what it is to be human.

In summary, contemporary anti-oppression movements are right to insist that nothing much can happen until the true self is in play. Their deficiency lies in underplaying or not seeing that the full stature of such a self is found only in offered victim-hood, the response characteristic of the person free enough to be fully identified with all the others. This is the way of those who, finding their life, are already beginning to lose it and who cannot be fully at peace until this surrender finds its consummation.

The mistake here, it might be suggested, is to try to connect victimhood with chosen victimhood, as the two simply do not belong together. A possible reply would be that what is at stake is the turning of victimhood into chosen victimhood. This is not merely a question of a change in mental approach: Etty volunteered to go to Westerbork, a transit camp for Auschwitz, and Jesus set his face towards Jerusalem. In so doing each was turning victimhood into chosen victimhood.

This way of putting the matter raises the bleak question of whether there are people who have had the freedom to choose victimhood taken away from them, i.e. people who have been *fully dehumanised?* It is hard to see how this terrifying possibility can be denied. This is a concern to which liberation theology seeks to sensitise a church still happy to be let off the hook in this area of oppression and deprivation. Was it perhaps in solidarity with such people that Jesus chose the course he did?

17

'I Have a Baptism . . .'

Christian faith has as its central act of worship the proclamation of a particular death, as if the world's whole destiny hinges upon it. The original context for faith was a bereavement, and there is an abiding strangeness about a faith that arises from the experience of a death; though the strangeness of this faith, as we find it charted in the New Testament, has nothing in common with that of a seance. There is further strangeness in the fact that this was a particularly nasty and ignominious death, without any of the obvious dignity or shape found in stories about martyrs or heroic sagas. Yet this is a death which, if the foundational witnesses are to be trusted, it is appropriate to proclaim, to celebrate, to live with a view to the consummation.

The New Testament books proclaim a memory, the memory of a man who both chose and dreaded a horrible and shapeless death. His dread is not disguised; yet his death is not remembered as a tragic necessity, nor yet as an act of resignation in the mood of the poet Keats, who found himself 'half in love with easeful Death' and wanted 'to cease upon the midnight with no pain'. No. Jesus' death is remembered as something positively chosen, an act of love, a freely chosen identification in compassion with the deepest human anguish. It is a choice of the worst, of the unthinkable, a self-determined immersion in the tortuous and tortured ambiguities of created life.

Here is the story of a man stretching life to its limit and so seeing death as the real limit. This man is alive to what death is and free to surrender his short-of-death life to it as the way to consummation. It is helpful here to recall Wittgenstein: 'Death is not an event of life. Death is not lived through.' Theologies of liberation and of healing will fall short of their creative potential if they fail fully to register this fact, that mind and body die. Short of this recognition they will yield to the temptation to continue to think in terms of preparing for a future which is not God's, a future which we can plan.

The resurrection does not undo the Passion, but makes it overtly scandalous. What the resurrection of Jesus gave to his chosen ones was precisely the sense of the overwhelming and abiding significance of his suffering and death, and that not merely in their lives but in the whole human story. All four evangelists give a preponderant place to the narrative of the Passion. Their conviction that Jesus has been raised does not lead them to lose interest in the form taken by his movement into death, but rather the reverse. All is interpretation, of course; but what is being interpreted, and offered to the neophyte as saving, is the death. Paul says that we are baptised into Jesus' death (Romans 6:3). The letter to the Colossians even tells its readers: 'You have died, and your life is hidden now with Christ in God' (Colossians 3:3). Identification with the death of Jesus could hardly go further.

'For it is the God who said, "Let light shine in darkness", who has shone in our hearts to give the light of the knowledge of the glory of God in the face of Christ' (2 Corinthians 4:6). A recent interpreter, D. F. Ford, points out that this face, which is neither separable from historical contingencies nor reducible to them, 'has also been dead. Yet it is seen as the manifestation of the glory of God, so that in future the glory of God and this death *cannot be thought* without each other' (my emphasis). The sense of an indissoluble conjunction between the death and the glory presents a sharp question. What is it that is specific to this death which has power to set at naught the worst that can happen?

In order to try to answer, or even properly to understand this question we need to recognise that our sense of death is distorted. Some effort is therefore necessary to pick up the resonance of the contrast between the vibrancy of Jesus' expectation of life through death and on the other hand 'death's magnet', that curious suction which the repressed thought of death otherwise exercises in the human adventure.

'I have a baptism with which to be baptised, and how I am straitened until it is accomplished' (Luke 12:50). Jesus refers here to his death. Because it is *his* death, with all that piety and ritual have subsequently projected onto it, it is all too easy to confine the experience of which he speaks exclusively to his story. This happens if we see Jesus as the one for whom everything

89

was different: it then becomes possible to say that death was like that for him because he was the redeemer, who had a special death to die and knew what it was about.

As good a way as any of beginning to recover awareness of the human normality of Jesus is to look *in ourselves* for a hint of the kind of consciousness of our own mortality which would give our death a role comparable to what Jesus saw in his. Do I ever get a glimpse of my death as the ending of limits? Do I ever sense it as something short of which I remain constricted? Is there in me a frustration which could be positively described as a yearning and negatively as an impatience with having to continue in the short-of-death condition? In other words is our death perhaps desirable to us in ways which have been largely excluded from our conscious dealings with one another? There is plenty of evidence that we can't live with a purely negative consciousness of death as that which gives the lie to all our achievements. We therefore get caught up in a flight from death which rules us all unawares.

Could it be the case that before this dynamic of denial comes into play a deeper and quite different sense of our death, hinted at in the questions in the last paragraph, has already been repressed? This would be the sense of death summarised in those words of Jesus about a baptism. The implication is that far from Jesus' approach to death being special in some unattainable way, it is simply that he has recovered for consciousness and as the direction of his life a sense of death as desirable which is in us all but largely obscured. This means that the difference made by the death of Jesus is in the making.

This approach to death must be sharply distinguished from the Freudian death-wish, which looks to death simply to end life. A death-wish in this sense is a wish to kill myself or the other, to bring things to an end, not the yearning to undergo the ending in the light of the promise. To see death as the end is quite different from seeing it as the ending of limits. The latter carries with it both terror and yearning.

Think of the anticipation of a major surgical operation, both desired and dreaded precisely because it will remove something which constricts my present state. Present constriction is familiar and habitual, to some extent dictating a pattern of life and a way of relating to things and people. What on earth will life be like without it? How will I cope? Wouldn't it be more sensible to carry on as I am? The transition to the new state is in any case, as far as I am concerned, hazardous in the extreme: my habitual ego-control system has to be relinquished as I hand over my body to the surgeon and my mind to the anaesthetic. In dying the factor of surrender to the unknown is total, with no prospect of the resumption of anything like our present network of sustaining relationships and interests.

It is this dissolution of the existing pattern which is threatening, whatever is to follow. The question Jesus' cry puts to us is whether being threatened is our fundamental response to the recognition of mortality, or whether it only appears to be so because the desire has been lost sight of. If Jesus had an unrepressed sense of death then instead of the one who sees death in a way no one else can we have him seeing death in a way everyone else can.

An unrepressed sense of death makes of it something at once desired and dreaded: desired in fulfilment of our destiny, dreaded as meaningless. In the story of Jesus there is evidence both of such desire and of such dread. His approach to death seems to spring from a place in himself where life and death are not at enmity. E. C. Hoskyns draws attention to a dialectic in the story between Jesus' movement of response to the immediate needs of others and his movement towards his death. It is dismaying that most theology is undisturbed by this dialectic. What do we suppose happened subsequently to those whom he healed, or fed, or delivered from evil spirits, or raised from the dead? How does his dealing with them relate to his journey to Jerusalem to die? If we miss the underlying movement into death this question will pass us by, despite the recorded dismay, fear and disapproval of the disciples.

It is worth adding that the cutting edge is blunted if we make the journey to Jerusalem a campaigning thrust. Then his death becomes no more than an unfortunate consequence of his stance towards life. It would be something Jesus risked rather than something he deliberately embarked upon in his whole way of living. To take that view would be to tell a very different and much less interesting story than the New Testament books, whatever else they differ on, consistently tell. Hoskyns claims that the wonders Jesus worked were in sign of his death, for death is where he was heading as 'he set his face towards Jerusalem', to the consternation of those who accompanied him. This journey to Jerusalem and death is remembered by early believers in the conviction that his way has become our destiny, our gift and our call.

That which is merely repressed does not disappear. In repression the yearning for death and the dread of it function obliquely and bewilderingly to disturb our short-of-death planning, hoping and sense of achievement. Instead of relating directly to our mortality we are ruled by its subterranean power. But if what is said here about Jesus is correct repression need not prevail, for in the completion of his open-eyed journey into life through death the healing truth about human mortality is brought out into the open.

Woody Allen said: 'I'm not afraid to die. I just don't want to be there when it happens!' It is not the death of Jesus, looked at on its own, which is distinctive. It is this death as the meaning of his life: as such it changes the shape of all human living and dying, for ever. It is, most strangely and yet most fittingly, the act of obedience towards which his whole life moves and in which the world is changed. In this man who journeys towards death we find someone who is living his own life. Only as we come upon and act out this freedom to live our own lives can death find its proper place, without morbidity or despair.

We can go his way. It seems reasonable to suppose that people who have had a brush with death may thereby have come more into touch with their own mortality than the rest of us. Certainly they often, in common with some others who are very close to death, express in their whole demeanour an enhanced sense of the wonder and preciousness of life, with no suggestion that the threat of death renders the present moment empty or futile. Much anxious caring observably falls away. All this would suggest the possibility that my death can be fully on my map as something which for all its aspect of terror is known in hope to be to do with the enhancement of life rather than its denial. There is, then, the capacity to relate to my own death as something to be desired. I suggest that identification with Jesus may bring this capacity out of hiding.

Jesus' approach to his death as something desired, as something without which his destiny would be unfulfilled, left his friends in total disarray. They could not cope with the deathward direction of this life which they could only interpret as life-affirming in an unredeemed sense, stopping short of death. There was for them an appropriate disillusionment. They came to see the force of Jesus' searing words to the sign-seekers that the only sign that mattered was the sign of Jonah: that is to say, himself dead, Jesus in the heart of the earth. That is how he became, in being raised from the dead, the burning centre of this universe, the one in whom our cosmos finds its godward meaning, no longer bound by death.

In Jesus the human flight from reality, symptomatically expressed in the multiple forms taken by the denial of death, is put into reverse. His death unlocks in humanity our freedom to obey. Through his death the Spirit is ready to open up in us that capacity freely to embrace our vocation epitomised in the words, 'Having nothing, we possess all things.' Our surprise at those who in face of death seem to become more vibrantly alive suggests that we are slow to acknowledge this reversal, and to become alive to the capacity in ourselves to enact it.

What difference would it make to our moral stance if the sense of our death as desirable were to emerge into full consciousness? With Jesus as the paradigm instance the whole of this book could be read as an attempt to answer that question, a sharper form of which might be 'What are we missing?'

As the sense of death as desirable begins to emerge we are freed to live fully in the present rather than being trapped by the present. This is the freedom not to be absolutely and exhaustively identified with the present form of our projects and relationships. Put positively it is the freedom to see and to rejoice in the fact that 'the form of this world is passing away'. It involves seeing the present not as static but as containing the past and inviting the future. It includes the capacity to receive the present as gift and the recognition that such a gift is given to be given. The difference between living and merely surviving is discovered in the very texture of our givenness, as the insecurities generated by creaturehood and finitude, turned inside out, are revealed as the place amongst us of the living God.

I have found no more powerful written witness to the spirit I seek to pinpoint here than this extract from a letter by Etty Hillesum written in Westerbork, a transit-camp for Auschwitz:

People here fritter their energy away on the thousand irksome details that grind us down every day; they lose themselves in detail and drown. That's why they get driven off course and find existence pointless. The few big things that matter in life are what we have to keep in mind; the rest can be quietly abandoned. And you can find those few big things anywhere, you have to keep rediscovering them in yourself so that you can be renewed. And in spite of everything you always end up with the same conviction: life is good after all . . . And that's what stays with me, even now, even when I'm about to be packed off to Poland with my whole family.

A review of the book in which this letter appears claims that the writer has become a symbol of 'saint-like resignation'. The use of such a ludicrously inappropriate and misleading category by a well-intentioned reviewer shows the difficulty of finding a language for what is at stake. The image of the saint as resigned tells its own sad tale, as if the alternative to being anxiously preoccupied with details is to be passive to your fate.

Theology also needs to hear a comparable cautionary word. Any failure to make Jesus' death central leaves us with a decentred theology, which may result in a preaching Jesus, an exemplary Jesus, a Jesus of confrontation, a justice-and-peace Jesus, or a blandly resurrected Jesus. All of these christologies make the mistaken assumption that the gospel is about some version of the good life rather than life with the living God. In thus distorting and diminishing Jesus we do drastically less than justice to ourselves and to the possibilities of our own vocation. It is a pity to isolate ourselves from the transformation-scene.

Part Four

18

Honour is the Subject of My Story

Weakness is readily taken for dishonour. We cover up whatever reminds us most insistently of our incompleteness, physically in terms of our sexual organs and psychologically in a myriad ways. We put immense energy into keeping our act together, or our show on the road. From our earliest years we are taught to live like this. It gets us into predicaments of which I shall consider two, one factual and the other fictional.

When my father came home from hospital I was standing by. Clad only in pyjamas and dressing-gown he emerged from the ambulance very weak and staggered to the nearest wall, against which he leaned for support. This was a very public moment of weakness. Yet far from any access of compassion I found myself despising him. Here was weakness where there should have been strength; this was my father, and it was shameful and even dishonourable that he should thus appear transparently and overwhelmingly weak. I wanted him to be strong not for his sake but for mine. I felt dishonoured by my father's weakness just as, I suggest, the disciples were by Jesus' weakness from the time of the onset of his Passion.

My second example is of a comparable sense of dishonour compellingly communicated in Shakespeare's *Julius Caesar*, when Cassius persuades Brutus to join the plot against Caesar's life. The play presents Brutus as the archetypal man of honour, a quality in him cunningly exploited by Cassius, who argues that it is shameful and shaming for a man of such glaring weakness as Caesar to rule the world. The disproportion between the public image and the particular person dishonours everybody. Cassius dwells on Caesar's failures in courage, once when swimming across the Tiber and once when ill with a fever on one of his campaigns. Caesar's nerve had failed when courage was to be expected. With arrant sexism he is even likened when feverish to 'a sick girl'. How then can it be right for him to rule? This speech voices an inability to live with weakness in a place where there should be only strength:

> ... we petty men
> creep under his huge legs, and peep about
> to find ourselves dishonourable graves.

What comes across to Brutus is moral outrage that those who can do something to change matters may choose not to. They are seen as thereby dishonoured and dishonourable. The honourable thing then by a very short step becomes the disposal of Caesar by those able to carry it out. A planned assassination becomes the course of honour which is to liberate from a dishonouring plight. Even Brutus' friendship with Caesar cannot shield him from an appeal couched in such terms.

The ancient world had a finely wrought sense of honour, which had pride of place in people's dealings with one another and with the gods. The New Testament by contrast offers Jesus, crucified under a curse outside the camp. He is presented, precisely in those wholly dishonourable circumstances, as the one who makes all the difference. We are suddenly in a world where honour has gone by the board and no longer has any place, at least if we look at the central figure. It is crucial to hold to this focus and to insist that in Jesus the furthest reaches of dishonour are attained. Otherwise we may well be distracted by extended consideration of the behaviour of the chief priests, Herod, Pilate, Judas and the eleven, all of whom could be said to have behaved less than honourably. But that isn't the point. They are merely playing their parts in relation to Jesus. What matters is what he is about, or where he is going. The others are functioning only in his slip-stream. The momentum is with him, clean contrary to the surface note of the story which has him being hustled from the priests to Pilate, from Pilate to Herod, and so on. He is throughout the only one who is going anywhere. The others are not so much criticised as left standing. There is no right or honourable response for them, for that frame of reference is rendered unavailable or inapplicable by what Jesus did.

Jesus chose his own dishonour. He entered deliberately into a situation where he signified and carried dishonour. It is fashionable in considering morality to speak of value-judgements, but all human judgements of value are criticised here. It is not simply that Jesus risked dishonour. He chose to be dishonour, to embody it and live it out to the disgraceful end. And he confirmed this choice not with dignity and restraint but in searing anguish, having signalled it with a donkey-ride.

The choice for Jerusalem, which was for Jesus a choice of exposure and weakness, is the hinge on which the whole story turns. Jesus did not fight for his life, still less for his honour. But nor was he passive to a fate seen as inexorable.

For Jesus the question of honour – his own or anyone else's – is turned upside down, or transcended, or seen to have no abiding reality. He had kept very disreputable company at times, and the choice he now made was in line with the logic of that company-keeping. His plunge into dishonour, his willed immersion, remains terrifying. In the New Testament he is presented as having come at this choice from a place in himself as yet totally inaccessible to his followers *in themselves*. 'He was beset', writes Peter Pritchard, 'with those wild, bedraggled desires to be with the lonely and the powerless'. Such desires left him free of the ethics of honour and so gloriously unbound by the compulsion to take offence. Such a person is subversive in a way no mere revolutionary could ever be.

Desire is at the core of this mystery: the unveiled desire of Jesus' whole being to be the epitome of loneliness and powerlessness, and therefore to be free of any shred of the dialectic of honour and dishonour that might prevent this. 'For the joy that was set before him he endured the cross, despising the shame' (Hebrews 12:2). No stoical endurance here. Jesus set the shame at nought by denying its category. He exposed its unreality by plunging into it. In this extraordinary exposure humanity came upon the place of the definitive exercise of the power of God in and with and for the love-child who is us all. Christ the King and all that, easily misses the point by turning the whole thing into a sort of imperial rally in disguise. What is lost sight of is the irony which the crucifixion proclaims at the heart of the whole business of honour and dishonour, praise and blame, kingship and non-kingship, priest and non-priest. All roles were put on the wobble, all heirarchies at risk from that time onwards.

'Honour and dishonour, praise and blame, what odds?' cries the exhilarated Paul (2 Corinthians 6:8), having an inkling at least at that moment of what it is to be in Christ. The burden of having to stand in and guard the tight network of honour, or of supporting it by colluding with our own exclusion from it, has been lifted. Paul also says we are to make up in our own bodies what is lacking in the sufferings of Christ. We too are to be that dishonour, that refuse, that thing of no account which Jesus became. We can be sufficiently awakened to our own humanity to be free to live in his spirit, beyond a distorted sense of honour. Jesus' ordeal is the empowering of us to live this way.

At this point a clarification is in order. So far this chapter has perhaps seemed to commend the choice of dishonour as such. But this choice would be just as imprisoning and alienating as the kind of concern with honour which is being stigmatised here. It would be equivalent to the choice of rebellion rather than conformity. No. What is being commended is the choice of *weakness*, which from the standpoint of unredeemed consciousness *is* dishonour. Only in living through weakness as dishonour can we come to the place where weakness is honour: 'Worthy is the Lamb who was slain.' Weakness embraced is honour.

It is all one story, to which we are intrinsic. From the time when Jesus' death entered the bloodstream of humanity the experience of neutrality in respect of his death is progressively revealed as illusory. The choice is to take the story further or not. To live this death or not. If not it still affects us, for it has happened, and to us all.

One form of evasion is to use the story of Jesus to set ourselves apart from and even over against the ambiguities of our present world, and in particular from the specific dishonourings that proceed. Our prayer can have as its unacknowledged heart the compulsion to declare that all is well when all is not well, or to hold back from the rough edge of life where moral signposts become elusive.

There are perhaps particular dangers in a current climate in which the concept of honour is unfashionable and the ceremony of innocence has little power over our oh-so-knowing minds. Our sophisticated but brittle culture sees itself as having got beyond that sort of thing. But all societies have a powerful if unacknowledged investment in particular images of what is worthy of honour and what is not. In the void created by our sterile knowingness honour re-emerges as the cult of achievement. Far from having unlearned the dialectic of honour and dishonour our society promotes a distinctive though largely covert way of perpetuating it. It is not that the worship of achievement deprives others of adequate income or employment, although that may sometimes be the case. Now, as ever, it is the power to control which is deemed honourable. The ruling imagery has as its most insidious consequence the reduction of 'non-achievers' of all sorts to the status of non-persons with nothing to hope for. This imagery reduces so many to nothing and then tells them it's their fault, a prescription for dull-eyed despair or extreme churlishness, both of which are not far to seek amongst us. That which is worthy of esteem is so narrowly defined that such rejection and these demoralised reponses are entailed. It is also worth sparing a thought for what the promoters of this culture are doing to themselves in the course of disowning so much in others.

This is very much a time to be absolutely explicit that the vindication of Jesus in degradation is the decisive declaration that each and every human person is of God, for God and for ever. This vindication reformulates human images of honour and dishonour. This reformulation can only become fully real for me through some degree of experienced and accepted victimhood. It is not mediated either by the culture of achievement and implied superiority, nor by the reactive cultivation of a sense of historic injustice and victimhood. These postures cannot satisfy our deepest yearning:

> We have all become like one who is unclean,
>   and all our righteous deeds are like a polluted garment.
> . . . for thou has hid thy face from us,
> and hast delivered us into the hand of our iniquities.
>
> (Isaiah 64:6–7)

Our best notions of honour and dishonour reveal from within their hollowness as they become 'like a polluted garment'. This is inescapable and salutary.

Karl Barth wrote in what is at first glance a vein similar to this when he claimed that there is only one authentic form of honour, that given by God in creation and election. But having allowed that particular cultural forms of honour may or may not coincide in part with true honour, Barth concludes that in practice we should be very slow to be convinced that there is a clash. It is remarkable how rapidly he moves from a radical opening assumption to this cagey conclusion. What he says was no doubt wise counsel in many circumstances, but it now looks amazingly ingenuous and potentially oppressive. I suspect most of us are like Barth in drawing back from the electrifyingly subversive claim Jesus embodies in choosing that which is named the dishonourable. To acclaim the slain lamb as worthy of all honour is to deconstruct in hope the reigning ideology.

19

Donkey-ride

I remember as a child on holiday on my uncle's small-holding in Ireland how disturbing was the braying of a donkey. This sound was beyond description or category, expressing a depth of restlessness, of pleading and of pain that I had not otherwise known. Then came G. K. Chesterton's poem, called simply 'The Donkey', to echo and enlarge my disturbance:

> With monstrous head and sickening cry
> And ears like errant wings,
> The devil's walking parody
> On all four-footed things.

Much later I read that the great Quaker George Fox had suppressed a dramatic incident when the authorised history of the first Quakers was composed. What had happened was that a leading Quaker rode into Bristol on a donkey, accompanied by followers, in conscious imitation of Jesus' entry into Jerusalem. For his pains this man was arrested and beaten within an inch of his life. Fox saw to it that this escapade did not appear in the official record of the movement he wished to commend. No doubt we can all identify with this desire to rule the donkey-rider's behaviour out of court in the interests of good order.

Then there is the suggestion that the Bible is best seen as a story of loss. The Israelites were given a land and lost it; they were given a monarchy and lost it; and so on. In this perspective Jesus appears as the culmination of the experience of loss. Our story about early Quakers recalls how the gospel presents Jesus' entry into Jerusalem. The hour of the donkey, a scene brimful of most bitter irony, not least because of the brittle acclamation of the bystanders. Then, immediately, he weeps over the city. Loss, loss, loss. Then the staccato flurry with the buyers and sellers in the Temple. Where is all this going? Nowhere but to his death. Jesus is the culmination of the experience of loss.

Commentaries properly insist that in taking his donkey-ride Jesus was acting out some words of the prophet Zechariah. This is offered as an explanation, as if it makes obvious sense of the incident. Yet to say, as the gospel does, that Jesus was acting out a prophecy makes his behaviour so threatening as to be off limits. To think otherwise is to imagine that the city fathers of Bristol would have been reassured to be told, of that early Quaker, 'It's all right – he's only imitating Jesus!' The fourth gospel is a help here in telling us that the disciples did not understand what was happening to Jesus. It could be surmised that they were still too full of messianic fantasies of power and status to be able to recognise either his wild surrender or the loss they were themselves undergoing.

Commentators also point out that Jesus' lamentation over the city is full of scriptural allusions. No doubt, and appropriately so, if the Bible is a story of loss. What we have at this moment is a man shaken to his depths by a sense of unimaginable loss and disintegration.

What then of the incident with the traders in the Temple, categorised by commentators as an eschàtological sign? This category effectively distances the episode, making of it no more than something that would have been intelligible in the world of ancient middle-eastern religion. If we leave it there we cut ourselves off from its immediate resonance, the swirl of desperation which characterises this moment in dynamic continuity with the donkey-ride and the lament. The whole sequence is at odds with normality: its movement is against the grain of half-awakened life. Under what conceivable rubric can we celebrate with loud hosannas a cataclysmic dissolution?

On the donkey Jesus brings nothing but himself into the city: no strategy of control, no secret messianic trump-card waiting to be played. His kingship is of surrender to the worst that can happen. There is no hint of that self-righteousness which is really self-withholding. The promoters of an ethical approach with non-violence as its heart perhaps fail to see that to stand in your own virtue is a posture of unloving.

The story of this man on a donkey seems to be saying: if it's kingship you're after this is the real thing – this unprotectedness, this seemingly reckless and yet trusting disregard of the best wisdom this world offers. Jesus' behaviour is subversive in a way which cuts much deeper even than that of the child who announced what everyone could see to be the case: that the emperor had no clothes. The donkey-ride goes further by presenting Jesus himself as king. Everything is in the melting-pot as he plunges into the maelstrom and is soon immersed and lost. It has to be so, for he knows what it is to be human in a world, religious and secular, then as now so heavily invested in grotesquely distorted and impoverished versions of humanity that the one who is fully alive cannot be allowed to live.

Jesus' wild way of entering the holy city shows him as beyond morality in any customary sense; beyond the weighing of consequences, beyond the art of the possible, beyond what we call our principles or, if we're pompous, our integrity. This form of self-exposure and self-offering, this readiness to be lost, so transcends all religious, moral and political categories that it seems still ahead of us, not as an ideal but as an awesome invitation to take the plunge. We encounter here the extraordinary power of someone who has become strong enough – or weak enough – to have abandoned all defences.

The power and the threat of Jesus lie in his capacity to call the true self of each of us out of repression and hiding. The whole thrust of his life and death is to awaken us, his brothers and sisters, to the place in ourselves which is open to the living God, with all the surprise and unlearning that awakening entails. In the extreme case this self has been so long buried and fled from that it has become the enemy. Ego is all, and nothing must disturb its supremacy. Short of this tragic extremity the self as lover nonetheless, and in the same way, invites the ending of reliance on carefully constructed ego-survival techniques, often compulsively sustained. Something has to give as crisis-point is reached.

From the point of view of our present theme we must hope to be ready to be as lost as Jesus chose to be. And to be thus ready means to let go of the myths of coping and of happiness which we construct to fend off our own dissolution. The Jesus of the donkey-ride, of the weeping and of the temple-scouring is disturbing and even frightening in exactly the same way that my true self is unsettling to everything about me that is unfree. My childhood reaction to the timeless cry of the Irish donkey was a portent.

In a human situation of self-rejection and universal captivity to the consequent mutually destructive behaviour there appears the one in whom this age-old dynamic is reversed. The one who knows himself loved without limit or condition, and who therefore can be nothing but love, seeks to awaken that in us which has kinship with him. This can only be done by way of surrender, in the way of the loss of everything.

W. B. Yeats set out to write a poem in memory of all who had influenced him, but found himself brought up short by the recollection of a particular person and his death:

> Some burn damp faggots, others may consume
> The entire combustible world in one small room
> As though dried straw, and if we turn about
> The bare chimney is gone black out
> Because the work had finished in that flare.
> Soldier, scholar, horseman, he,
> As 'twere all life's epitomé.
> What made us dream that he could comb grey hair?

'All life's epitomé'. This is the very least we would want to say of what Jesus was for the first disciples. This is a minimal version of the claim made for Jesus by the evangelists and other New Testament writers. If for Yeats the memory of his friend's death 'took all my heart for speech', must we not allow a comparable reaction in the friends of Jesus, complicated by the unexpected, ignominious and inexplicable nature of his Passion and death?

It is to be expected that not all aspects of the response would be equally convincing. Recall for instance those Christians who were thrown into confusion by the fact that some of their number had died. They had come to imagine death as out of court for followers of Jesus, and so had to find reasons for these deaths. Scholars observe that many early Christians reasoned thus because they thought Jesus was about to come again. But this is to draw attention to a symptom as if it were self-explanatory. To think of Jesus as presently absent but liable at any moment to return is a frame of mind only explicable as a very early stage in the corporate negotiation of the shock of his loss. In the nature of the case such expectations could not survive indefinitely in their original freshness. But some forms of eucharistic devotion later came to perform a comparable function, providing the substitute presence of a Lord understood as otherwise simply and unbearably absent. Likewise with some forms of the classical Protestant doctrine of the preached word as the authoritative presence of Christ. The human psyche in its religious vein is almost endlessly resourceful in providing sops to our insecurity.

Much of our talk of Jesus' resurrection and divinity is regressive, evading the shock by putting him in the pantheon, as a bigger and better God than any of the others. 'Thus', writes Sebastian Moore, 'we resurrect for our security the God whose death is our salvation.' But despite this recurrent tendency to regress, the centre of Christian revelation is not 'man knowing himself in a meaningful world', but

> man dissolved in death, reduced to the death that ever gave the lie to the human myth of a friendly and humanly meaningful world out there. The world is not a stage but a process in which man is engulfed and lost, and this humanly unbearable truth is the place of God's coming to us in the risen Christ.

We must therefore take the disjunction seriously, allowing ourselves to experience to the full whatever form of dislocation hits us. In just such ordeals lies our precious bane, having to do with the honing of us into our true identity in God. Always the promise is there, the gift is there, the invitation is there. But the burgeoning of these is only in and through loss. There has to be surrender, the risk of intimacy with God. We need to become less and less defended, less and less identified with our own ideas of God, more and more attentive to the promptings of the Spirit and to the other person's story, spoken or unspoken, whoever or whatever that person may be, that we may together receive the abundance.

Epilogue

I

The sweet promise is an open horizon, blue sky, the clearest brightness of day. Here the tragedy is sunlit, sharply etched as such in the memory: North Sea a gleaming mill-pond, or shimmering west country early morning, hot. Bright backdrop for cataclysm.

Then the labyrinth. This unnerving sense of loss of bearings, loss of context, loss of purpose. ' . . . and there was darkness over the whole land.' This is the ordeal, necessary if the meaning of the shining tragedy is to be declared – or, rather, if the tragedy is to radiate its meaning along the sinews of the world.

II

Insecurity asks, 'What if the worst happens, as it surely will?' Faith says, 'The worst has happened, and its meaning is being worked out in the plumbing of the depths and the scaling of the heights.' Insecurity presents an image of final disaster, while faith speaks of the harrowing of hell. 'Fear not to enter hell, for Christ your Saviour has harrowed it.' Hell, the projected place where we put all the evil we can't cope with in ourselves, is thus brought near, reactivated within us and turned over.

We used to comfort ourselves by saying that, while we perhaps had to believe that hell existed, we didn't have to hold that anyone ever went there. In speaking thus we had forgotten Jesus, and by implication everyone else, for his story is ours: through hell to heaven. You have to have forgotten not only Jesus but a great deal of your own experience to be able to doubt either hell or its inhabiting. Equally you have to be in full flight from present reality to place hell firmly and exclusively after death, and to picture it as a sealed-off alternative to heaven. Such literalism misses the meaning.

Annotated Bibliography

Listed here are only those books, papers and poems which have had a direct and identifiable influence on this work. My debts are considerably more comprehensive.

Barth, K., *Church Dogmatics*, vol. III, part 4 (T. and T. Clark, Edinburgh, 1961), §54.2 Parents and Children; §56.3 Honour.

Becker, E., *The Denial of Death* (Collier Macmillan 1975). Cogent anatomy of the repressed sense of death as endemic and destructive.

Bion, W., *Experiences in Groups and other papers* (Tavistock Publications 1961). Insights into group dynamics, especially about dependency.

Bolton, J. D. P., *Glory, Jest and Riddle* (Duckworth 1973). Jesus' disruption or transcendence of the ancient world's sense of honour forms a keystone in the development of the human spirit.

Bonhoeffer, D., *Ethics* (SCM Press 1978). The first chapter, poignantly left unfinished, claims that Christian ethics begins with the unlearning of the knowledge of good and evil. Later come villains and saints (p. 46).

Bruce, F. F., *The Hard Sayings of Jesus* (Hodder and Stoughton 1983). An example, alas, of how vast learning and comprehensive scope can fail to prevent the sayings losing their cutting edge.

Chesterton, G. K., *Collected Poems* (Methuen 1954). This collection includes 'The Donkey' and 'The Ballad of the White Horse' which, though seriously flawed, includes the vignette of King Alfred quoted in chapter 9, besides other wondrous passages.

Cupitt, D., *The New Christian Ethics* (SCM Press 1988). Pays no serious attention to the text and so makes Jesus a late-twentieth-century post-existentialist moraliser.

Dubay, T., *Happy Are You Poor* (Dimension Books, Denville N.J., 1981). Stresses questions of identity and expectation which point beyond any facile polarisation of rich and poor.

Dykstra, C., *Vision and Character: a Christian Educator's Alternative to*

Kohlberg (Paulist Press, New York, 1981). Regards most theories of moral development as being about social adjustment, not morality. Commends mystery-encountering rather than problem-solving.

Ford, D. F., 'Tragedy and Atonement', in *Christ, Ethics and Tragedy: Essays in Honour of Donald MacKinnon*, edited by K. Surin (Cambridge University Press 1989), pp.117–30. The glory of God and the death of Jesus simply *cannot be thought* of apart from each other.

Fuchs s.j., J., *Christian Morality: the Word Becomes Flesh* (Gill and Macmillan, Dublin, 1987). The ideas summarised towards the end of my chapter 5 occur *passim* in this difficult and execrably translated but rewarding collection.

Harvey, N. P., *Death's Gift: Chapters on Resurrection and Bereavement* (Epworth Press 1985). The disciples' experience of the risen Jesus, and their conviction of his saving role, is only intelligible in the context of their continuing bereavement.

Hauerwas, S., *A Community of Character: Toward a Constructive Christian Social Ethic* (University of Notre Dame Press 1981). Whose story are we living?

Haughton, R., *The Transformation of Man* (Geoffrey Chapman 1968). Formation must precede transformation, and is the necessary ground of it.

Hill, C., *The World Turned Upside Down* (Penguin 1984). Tells of Fox's suppression of the story of James Nayler's Bristol donkey-ride and its brutal aftermath, among much else about lively 'sectaries'.

Hillesum, E., *Etty: a Diary 1941–43* (Jonathan Cape 1983). Records her shift from living an accidental life into an empowering sense of a particular destiny.

Hillesum, E., *Letters From Westerbork* (Grafton Books 1988). Flashes of light in extreme darkness. We are not simply the prisoners of environment or circumstance.

Hoskyns, E. C. and N. Davey, *Crucifixion–Resurrection: the Pattern of the Theology and Ethics of the New Testament* (S.P.C.K. 1981). Chapter 8 for the double movement in the story of Jesus: towards others' needs and towards his death. Chapter 9 for the gospel's redefinition of all relationships. It is not that the gospels 'contain here or there a hard saying. These hard sayings correspond with and explain the action of Jesus himself' (p. 236).

Hudson, S. D., *Human Character and Morality* (Routledge and Kegan Paul 1986). Sees the search for *the* moral point of view, wholly neutral and disinterested, as initiated in part at least by *fear* of what morality would be like if such a point of view did not exist. This diagnosis is applied to 'enlightened' thinkers such as Kant and Hume; but it is not dissimilar to Becker's suggestion that moral bigotry stems from a fear of not being able to control life and death.

Hull, J. M., *Touching the Rock* (S.P.C.K. 1990). His thought awakened me to the Bible as a story of loss; but this more recent work is on a connected subject, his experience of being blind.

Kierkegaard, S., *The Sickness unto Death* (Princetown University Press 1983). The opposite of sin is not virtue but faith.

Kierkegaard, S., *Fear and Trembling* (Penguin 1985). The necessity for the teleological suspension of ethics in the interests of faith in the living God.

Laing, R. D., *The Divided Self* (Penguin 1965); *The Politics of Experience* (Penguin 1967). His questions about the true and false self abide, despite the fact that this maverick psychiatrist is not even a footnote in the textbooks these days.

McDonagh, E., *Doing the Truth* (Gill and Macmillan, Dublin, 1979), chapter 12. Jesus as the bringer of scandal.

Matura, T., *Gospel Radicalism: the Hard Sayings of Jesus* (Gill and Macmillan, Dublin, 1978). The 'ism' is the give-away. Full of interesting things but succumbs to the moralising tendency.

Merton, T., *The Wisdom of the Desert: Sayings from the Desert Fathers of the Fourth Century* (Sheldon Press 1961). The most important voyage of discovery is across the abyss that separates us from ourselves.

Miller, A., *The Drama of the Gifted Child* (Basic Books, New York, 1981). Strong on the genesis and perpetuation of the second-hand life enlarged upon in my chapter 16, where the formerly suicidal woman comes from Miller. Originally published as *Prisoners of Childhood*.

Moore, S., *God is a New Language* (Darton, Longman and Todd 1967), part 2, chapter 3. The centre of Christian revelation is 'man dissolved in death'.

Moore, S., *The Crucified is No Stranger* (Darton, Longman and Todd 1977). The true self as my crucified victim.

Moore, S., *The Inner Loneliness* (Darton, Longman and Todd 1982), pp. 97–9. Jesus has an unrepressed sense of death.

Moore, S., *Let This Mind Be In You: the Quest for Identity through Oedipus to Christ* (Darton, Longman and Todd 1985), chapter 28. The universal condition of arrested development serves as a contemporary description of original sin.

Parker, D. C., *Codex Bezae: an Early Christian Manuscript and its Text* (Cambridge University Press 1991). The whole book, and chapter 16 in particular, offers background to the remarks in my introduction about the biblical text. This work exemplifies Derrida's picture of work done on the margins causing a tremor at the centre.

Rivkin, E., *What Crucified Jesus?* (SCM Press 1984). An outstanding example of the work of those who pursue this type of question, mentioned in the opening paragraph of my chapter 10.

Sanders, E. P., *Jesus and Judaism* (SCM Press 1985). Clear view of what in the reported sayings of Jesus would have been offensive, and what would not, to first-century Jews.

Sanders, J. T., *Ethics in the New Testament: Change and Development* (SCM Press 1975). Misguided expectation of imminent end dictates New Testament ethics.

Smail, D., *Illusion and Reality: the Meaning of Anxiety* (Dent 1984). Clear picture of the power of prevalent socio-political myths of success and happiness to drive people into illusion and then insist that it is their fault.

Sobrino, J., *Christology at the Crossroads* (SCM Press 1978). The resurrection makes the Passion overtly scandalous.

Thomas, R. S., 'Song at the Year's Turning', in *Selected Poems 1946–1968* (Bloodaxe Books 1986; © R. S. Thomas, reproduced by kind permission). This includes the account of the fate of Morgan the Minister quoted in chapter 9, which could be taken as a parabolic expression of the wisdom of Jesus' 'hard saying', 'Do not confront one who is evil.'

Yeats, W. B., 'The Second Coming' and 'In Memory of Major Robert Gregory' can be found in his *Collected Poems* (Macmillan 1955). The former poem is relatively familiar; the latter, quoted in my final chapter, gives incomparable expression to the abiding shock of unexpected, abrupt and total loss.

A Note on Unpublished Work

Barthelémy, D. I owe to his unpublished lectures on the Old Testament two key ideas. Human hope must be brought to nothing before theological hope can flourish. The dynamic in human life from terror to love proceeds by way of fear of the Lord.

Pritchard, P. His unpublished 'Advent Meditation' speaks of Jesus' wild and bedraggled *desires* to be with the lonely and powerless.